trotman

REAL LIFE ISSUES:
ADDICTIONS

D0993747

REAL LIFE ISSUES

Real Life Issues are self-help guides offering information and advice on a range of key issues that matter to teenagers. Each book defines the issue, probes the reader's experience of it and offers ways of understanding and coping with it. Written in a lively and accessible style, Real Life Issues aim to demystify the areas that teenagers find hard to talk about, providing honest facts, practical advice, inspirational quotes, positive reassurance, and guidance towards specialist help.

Other titles in the series include:

Real Life Issues: Bullying
Real Life Issues: Confidence & Self-Esteem
Real Life Issues: Coping with Life
Real Life Issues: Eating Disorders
Real Life Issues: Money
Real Life Issues: Sex and Relationships
Real Life Issues: Stress

REAL LIFE ISSUES:
ADDICTIONS

Stephen Briggs

Real Life Issues: Addictions
This first edition published in 2005 by Trotman and Company Ltd
2 The Green, Richmond, Surrey TW9 1PL

Reprinted 2005

Editorial and Publishing Team
Author Stephen Briggs
Editorial Mina Patria, Editorial Director; Rachel Lockhart, Commissioning Editor;
Catherine Travers, Managing Editor; Bianca Knights, Assistant Editor
Production Ken Ruskin, Head of Pre-press and Production;
James Rudge, Production Artworker
Sales and Marketing Deborah Jones, Head of Sales and Marketing
Advertising Tom Lee, Commercial Director
Managing Director Toby Trotman

Designed by XAB

British Library Cataloguing in Publication Data
A catalogue record for this book is available from the British Library

ISBN 0 85660 992 7

Typeset by Tradespools Publishing Solutions
Printed and bound in Great Britain by
Cromwell Press, Trowbridge, Wiltshire

CONTENTS:

'... you need other people to help you overcome addictive behaviour and to avoid becoming addicted.'

REAL LIFE ISSUES:
Addictions

ABOUT THE AUTHOR

Stephen Briggs works in the Tavistock Clinic's Adolescent Department.
The Department provides psychoanalytic psychotherapy for young
people with emotional and mental health difficulties. It also trains a
wide range of people working in the UK and internationally in the field
of mental health issues for young people. Stephen has written books
for healthcare professionals about young people and infants.

REAL LIFE ISSUES:
Addictions

ACKNOWLEDGEMENTS

I am grateful to my colleagues in the Adolescent Department for the help they have given me over many years, and to my family for being so supportive. I would also like to acknowledge the contribution of the people I have worked with as students and patients.

This book contains a number of case studies, all of which have been disguised and fictionalised to preserve confidentiality and anonymity.

INTRODUCTION

This book provides information about addictive activities and behaviour. Addictions are serious personal problems which reduce your chances of making the most of your life and undermine your physical and emotional health. During your teenage years you can be very vulnerable to beginning patterns of behaviour which can lead to addiction, and some teenagers may become addicted. Knowing about the causes of addictive behaviour can help you make informed choices which mean you are able to avoid the damaging effects of addiction.

Most people think of drugs as causing addiction. It is true that the misuse of drugs is one main reason why people get addicted. But there are also other important background reasons. People who get addicted have problems with managing their emotions, and feel disappointed or let down in relationships with others. This book will help you understand how emotions and the way you relate to others are important for your health. It will show that in order to get help for an addiction you need to change not only your behaviour, but also your relationships and your ways of dealing with your feelings. It provides you with information that will help you make choices about your lifestyle, and assess how vulnerable you might be to addictions.

There are many forms of addiction: as well as the obvious ones like drug misuse, drinking alcohol and smoking, there are activities like gambling, eating too much or too little, excessive exercising and excessive internet surfing, all of which can become addictions. Each of them will be discussed in this book.

The aim of the book is to help you know more about addictions, to understand the ways they can get started and how they affect your life – always for the worse. One problem for people who get addicted is that they have tried to solve problems without turning to other people for support. This book shows that you need other people to help you overcome addictive behaviour and to avoid becoming addicted. Self-help is about realising the importance of relating to and relying on others!

WHAT IS ADDICTION?
How does it start? Who is likely to become addicted?

Being addicted is a problem that needs to be taken very seriously. It is important to understand what an addiction is, how addictions start and who is likely to get addicted. Help for addiction is available, and it is important to know what kind of help to seek and how to go about getting it – so read on! Knowing about the nature of addiction may mean you can avoid developing one – and this is always the best form of help!

WHAT DOES ADDICTION MEAN?

Addiction involves **regular** and **dependent** participation in an addictive activity. Being dependent means that the activity cannot be easily regulated – you feel that it is beyond your control. So addiction means that someone is tied to a way of behaving. We say someone has a 'habit' because they carry out a pattern of behaviour which is repetitive and which they feel they cannot control. When someone is addicted, they feel that they cannot leave their habit alone or stop it without it having a harmful effect on them. They have an addictive state of mind.

FACT BOX

Addiction is a Latin word which means being 'tied to' or 'making a bond with' something.

So an addict has a strong, even intense, *attachment* to the addictive activity, and feels unable to break this bond. Because the attachment is so strong, being addicted means continuing with or failing to reduce your involvement in the activity, despite having bad feelings about it. You know that the addiction has negative consequences, and that it is harming yourself and others, but you are unable or unwilling to take notice of these negative effects.

Addiction is a social problem because its effects can be severely damaging both to yourself and to others. Its effects include:

- Damaging your physical and mental health
- Causing you financial loss
- Making you become socially marginalised (meaning that other people treat you as insignificant, exclude you or ignore you)
- Getting you into trouble with the law
- Damaging your relationships with friends, work colleagues, parents and partners.

ADDICTIVE ACTIVITIES

Although we often think about addiction as being about getting hooked on drugs, in fact you can get addicted to a range of activities. Some of these activities involve taking a chemical into the body – as in drugs, drink and smoking. Others do not require a chemical intake, but consist instead of an activity or behaviour which is repetitive and preoccupying or **compulsive**. These activities include gambling, some forms of dieting and exercising. Recently, new addictions have also emerged, such as getting 'addicted' to the internet.

These substances and activities are listed in the box below. The left-hand list requires taking a substance into the body, and the list on the right is of addictions which involve a pattern of behaviour without a chemical intake.

Addictive substances and activities

Alcohol   Dieting
Caffeine   Exercising
Cannabis   Gambling
Cocaine   Internet
Ecstasy   Sex
Heroin   Shopping
LSD   TV
Morphine
Nicotine

Vote Now!

Can you decide which of the substances or activities in these two columns are the most addictive *in your view*? Make a 'top ten' from the list (1 being the most addictive).

Now compare your views with a friend's. Do you agree, or disagree?

If you disagreed with your friend's answers, this might be because you have different positions, attitudes, emotions or experiences – it does *not* mean that one of you is wrong. We will see that what makes an activity 'addictive' depends on a number of factors, not just on an objective or 'correct' view of how dangerous it is. Read on to find out more!

ADDICTION IS A PROCESS

Addiction does not happen overnight – it is a process that develops over time. In order to understand addiction we have to identify the different stages in the process of becoming addicted. It is important to distinguish carefully between addictive behaviour and taking part in an activity in a way that does not carry much risk of addiction. This can be illustrated by using gambling and alcohol as examples.

It would clearly be unhelpful to describe everyone who drinks alcohol as an addict. Some people have a glass of wine with a meal; others have an occasional drink. This is quite different from the kind of excessive consumption of alcohol described by some people who admit to being addicts. It is the same with gambling. Some people, for example, have a small bet once a year on the Grand National horse race. Others buy a lottery scratch card now and again. This does not compare with the kind of gambling behaviour which takes over the person's life. In a similar way, many young people experiment with drugs, but very few become addicted.

So addiction means getting involved in a particular activity **to excess**. There are three elements which make up *excessive* involvement. They are:

■ **Frequent or regular engagement** in the activity, so that a pattern of behaviour emerges
■ **High quantities** – this might mean drinking large amounts quickly, or spending large sums of money on gambling, or moving from soft to hard drugs, or taking drugs in combinations

■ **Preoccupation with the activity**, so that it seems all-important. This might mean thinking about the activity a lot, wanting to do it again and not wanting to stop.

Confessions of an Opium Eater

A famous example of an addict in the past is that of the writer Thomas De Quincey, who lived in the nineteenth century. In 1821 he wrote a book, *Confessions of an English Opium Eater*, about his addiction to opium. In it he said:

'From this day the reader is to consider me as a regular and confirmed opium-eater, of whom to ask whether on any particular day he had or had not taken opium would be to ask whether his lungs had performed respiration or the heart fulfilled its functions.'

Although De Quincey lived a long time ago, his words clearly show what it means to be addicted. For him, taking opium is as regular, basic and vital to his way of life as breathing. The idea of stopping taking opium seems not to occur to him, though elsewhere in his writing he does refer to the torment he felt when he could not stop taking the drug.

De Quincey's addiction, shown in the box above, is at the extreme end of addiction. Because getting addicted is a process, there are points along the way where the activity has less of a hold and it is easier to stop. But it might be harder to stop earlier in the addictive process, because the harmful side is not so severe. This might sound like a contradiction, but think of it like this: if you don't feel you are doing any harm to yourself, or you *think* you can stop before you do harm to yourself, you won't be so worried that you feel you ought to stop now. You might put off stopping for the future. We know for example that people are more likely to stop smoking if they are afraid of getting ill from it.

Recovery

Recovery from addiction is also a process, and the more deeply attached someone is to the addictive activity, the more lengthy the recovery process will be. Just as you don't get addicted overnight, you don't recover that quickly either. Being addicted is very serious as it affects all parts of your life and means that there is something deeply wrong. Recovery from serious addiction is possible – but it is difficult and involves a lot of work. It means facing what has gone wrong in your life. Giving up an addiction is always painful – emotionally, as well as physically. Separating from your intense attachment to the addiction is emotionally a very difficult thing to do because of the emotional or psychological dependence on the addiction. We can look at this more closely by seeing what it means to be dependent on an addictive activity.

DEPENDENCY

Being attached to the addictive activity without being able to stop or take notice of its negative effects shows **dependency**. But being dependent is essential in life. We are always, to some extent, **dependent on others**, meaning that we rely on and trust others to help us when we are in need. We develop attachments to others to provide us with a sense of well-being and confidence. The problem is that being **dependent on addictive activities** alters this kind of attachment, meaning that instead of relying on help from other people, you depend on an activity, which is in fact harmful. Remember what De Quincey said – it is just like breathing. But breathing air is healthy – an addiction is not. Dependency on addiction is unreliable and damaging. Whatever you think you would gain from the addictive activity backfires – in the end, the addiction is always harmful.

There are two types of dependency: **physical** and **psychological**. All addictions involve psychological dependency, and some drugs also create physical dependency.

Physical dependency

Physical addiction is the way that the body comes to rely on a drug. The reaction to stopping using this drug induces a painful physical state (known as **withdrawal**), strong cravings when the substance is not available, and a sense that balance can only be restored by taking the drug again.

Some drugs – especially opiates like heroin or opium – have to be taken regularly, not to achieve the original feeling gained from taking them, but just *in order to feel normal*. So as you become familiar with an addictive activity, you have to do it in greater amounts and more often in order to achieve the desired effects. When this happens we say that you have developed a **tolerance**.

Withdrawal symptoms

Tony Adams, the former Arsenal and England footballer, gives an open and honest account of his addiction, including the effects of withdrawing from his physical dependency on alcohol. In his book *Addicted* (1998, Collins Willow publishers, London) written with Ian Ridley he describes how he spent 36 hours in bed alternating between hot sweats and cold shivers. This is a very graphic account of being physically addicted, where the pains of withdrawing are located in the body.

Psychological dependency

There are always personal reasons for getting involved in addictive activities. People having a hard time in their lives emotionally can feel the need for a way out of current difficulties and painful experiences. If good support from others has not been available, or if you have been traumatised by difficult events, drugs and addictive activities might *seem* to provide an answer to your problems. We say that using drugs in this way is 'self-medicating', meaning that drugs are used as though they are prescribed medicines, in order to deal with the pains and miseries of life.

'… drugs and addictive activities might seem to provide an answer to your problems.'

Taking drugs can be attractive to many people who, for a range of reasons, find it difficult to face the sometimes painful – or often ordinary, boring and unexceptional – realities of life. Being able to bear disappointments and miseries from time to time is an important part of being human – but some people find these feelings cannot be endured at all, and this is when an escape through drugs and other activities can lead to an addiction.

The popularity of some addictive activities is connected with a wish to experience pleasure. Certain states of pleasurable feeling are associated with drug use, including:

■ The relaxation, or reduction in tension felt when taking alcohol or cannabis
■ The rush of pleasure associated with heroin or cocaine

■ The excitement and tension of gambling
■ The runners' 'high'.

But these pleasures are short-lived and do not solve problems. If you are reliant on escaping from reality and needing to use addictive activities to obtain pleasure then you have an addictive state of mind. This makes it difficult to control your addictive behaviour. It leads to becoming trapped in a vicious circle in which, being convinced that the drug or activity is the *only* way to feel pleasure, you return to it repeatedly to try to obtain the desired feelings and, at the same time, to avoid or reduce an unwanted experience. Seeking pleasure in the activity and avoiding unpleasant realities are two sides of the same coin in the life of the addict.

The vicious circle of addiction

The vicious circle of addiction is an important consequence of dependency. To start with, the addictive activity is used to bring about pleasant feelings and avoid unpleasant ones. But as time goes by, a greater involvement is needed to continue to experience the original pleasant feelings. Then the harmful effects of the addiction lead to new kinds of unhappiness, and the addict gets more involved in the addiction to try to reduce unhappiness and avoid these new and unpleasant realities – so in this way the addiction increases. In Chapter 4, you can read about the vicious circle of addiction in more detail.

'Seeking pleasure in the activity and avoiding unpleasant realities are two sides of the same coin in the life of the addict.'

The vicious circle of addiction

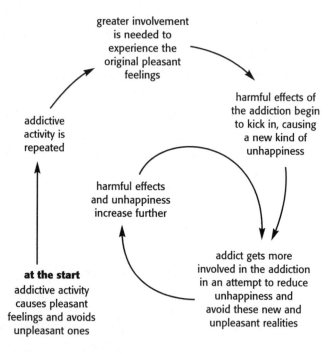

greater involvement
is needed to
experience the
original pleasant
feelings

harmful effects of
the addiction begin
to kick in, causing
a new kind of
unhappiness

addictive
activity is
repeated

harmful effects
and unhappiness
increase further

at the start
addictive activity
causes pleasant
feelings and avoids
unpleasant ones

addict gets more
involved in the addiction
in an attempt to reduce
unhappiness and
avoid these new and
unpleasant realities

To explore the issue of dependency in more depth, have a look at
Chapter 7, which goes into more detail about the different kinds of
dependency.

So addiction is the consequence of becoming psychologically
dependent on addictive activities. This means that it is important to
find an addict's social and psychological *motives* for becoming involved
in the addictive activity, as well as looking at the activity itself. For
information on some of the social and psychological reasons that

young people can start getting involved in addictive activities, see Chapter 7.

WHO IS SUSCEPTIBLE TO ADDICTION?

Most people who become addicts start their addictive behaviour in adolescence. Many young people try drugs, alcohol, cigarettes and gambling, and many are preoccupied with food, diet and exercise. Most do not come to any harm – but some, through continuing with these activities, experience addiction and other harmful effects. This means that some people are **vulnerable** to the development of an addiction. Others face similar difficulties, but are **resilient** and able to overcome the difficulties without harm. People who are susceptible to

FACT BOX

Vulnerability and resilience
Vulnerability does not mean 'weakness'. It is the term used to describe the way that circumstances and personal experiences lead someone to be more open or susceptible to harmful effects. Some people are more sensitive to painful experiences than others and find it harder to get over setbacks. Resilience means having the ability to overcome difficulties – to bounce back from adversity and to face realities.

addiction are likely to feel that life's difficulties are too much to bear, and to believe that they can find a 'quick fix' to solve them.

Factors which can make you vulnerable to developing addictions are explored in more detail in Chapter 7.

SOCIETIES AND ADDICTION

No society exists without addictive drugs and activities, though these vary between cultures and over time. Drugs have been used for at least 13,000 years! All societies legalise some drugs and practices and forbid others. Alcohol is the obvious example of a drug which is legal today in some cultures (for example in the West) and illegal in others (for example in some Muslim countries). Various forms of gambling have also always existed, and have been authorised in different countries. The status of cigarette smoking has changed over time: in the early twentieth century smoking was fashionable, but today in Europe and the USA it is only semi-legalised, and it is strongly discouraged. There is now a debate about banning cigarette smoking in public places. On the other hand, cannabis is becoming more acceptable in legal terms: for example in Amsterdam it is legalised, and in the UK it has recently been downgraded as an illegal drug from a 'Class B' to a 'Class C' drug. (This means that although cannabis is still considered dangerous in the UK, it is thought to be less dangerous than some other drugs, like cocaine and heroin.)

'No society exists without addictive drugs and activities.'

The variation in the way that different societies and different generations authorise or ban addictive activities means that some addictive drugs are more culturally acceptable than others, at different times and in different places. So some drugs and activities are thought to be more dangerous or less dangerous depending on the time and the place. This means that the time and place are important considerations in shaping people's attitudes to different addictive activities.

Although we must recognise that it is subject to change, the legal status of a drug helps to highlight whether it is dangerous to health. The most seriously damaging drugs – such as heroin – are illegal. Some activities are legal, but have potential dangers. For example, alcohol (for adults) and gambling are legalised in the UK – but, when misused, they can be dangerous. So people can also get addicted to excessive drinking and gambling, even though these activities in themselves are not illegal.

HOW DO YOU FEEL ABOUT ADDICTIONS?

Understanding more about addictive behaviour and addictive states of mind is very important both in preventing addiction and helping recovery. It will be helpful to identify where you think you are in the addictive process, and whether you experience addictive states of mind. You can do this by thinking about the issues raised, seeing if any of the case studies describes an issue you can identify with, and considering the questions you are encouraged to ask yourself throughout the book. When you do this, share your responses with friends.

Reading this book will help you adopt some essential coping strategies. Try not to treat it as a quick fix, because quick fixes usually cause problems rather than solving them. Instead, try to use the knowledge you gain from reading the book to help you understand addiction and understand yourself. Remember:

▨ Talk to others and share reading the book with peers and trusted adults

▨ If you *are* engaged in addictive activities, ensure you have professional support and follow the advice and treatment given by your professional helpers. Obtain professional support immediately if you don't have it – for more information on how to do this, see Chapter 8

▨ If you are worried that you *might* be getting involved in addictive activities, share your thoughts about this and use the book to help you talk to others. Don't decide for yourself without checking with people you trust!

▨ Use the suggestions in the book to check out other relevant sources of information.

CHAPTER TWO:

THE CAUSES OF DRUG ADDICTION
How and why do people get involved?

In this chapter we look at some of the general issues surrounding drug use and misuse. We look at how and why young people get involved with drugs. In Chapter 3 we will focus in on the specific effects of different drugs.

YOUNG PEOPLE AND DRUGS – WHO GETS INVOLVED?

Let us be clear: most young people who try drugs do so briefly and safely, limiting these experiences to alcohol and 'soft' drugs like cannabis. Experimenting with drugs is a part of being young – even politicians have done it! On the other hand, there is great concern about young people taking drugs and alcohol because a small number of the people who try them go on to develop problems. These include addiction, and putting yourself in a very vulnerable position where you can be physically or emotionally hurt, or even killed.

Let us look at the statistics. Most surveys show that about 38 per cent of people between 11 and 15 have taken drugs or drunk alcohol.

Young people taking drugs, smoking and drinking

Statistics gathered by the National Centre for Social Research every year measure how many teenagers aged between 11 and 15 take drugs, drink alcohol and smoke cigarettes.

In 2003, their results showed that, out of all young people between 11 and 15:

21% had taken drugs in the last year
(an increase from 20% in 2002 and 2001)

12% had taken drugs in the last month
(the same proportion as in 2002 and 2001)

9% were regular smokers
(a decrease from 10% in 2002)

25% had drunk alcohol in the last week
(a small increase from last year's figure of 24%)

The government wants to reduce the number of young people who start drinking, smoking and taking drugs but there are no signs that this is happening. These activities remain popular for a large number of people.

From the many people who take drugs, it is difficult to work out who will be unharmed by this experience and who will be vulnerable to becoming addicted. We need to look at the main factors that lead young people into difficulty with drug use. On the practical side, this means looking at exactly what an addictive drug is, at the process of how people move from taking soft drugs to hard drugs, and at how they eventually become addicted. On the emotional side, this means looking at the underlying reasons why people take addictive drugs in the first place, and why they continue to take them.

WHAT IS AN ADDICTIVE DRUG?

Addiction is often associated with illegal hard drugs such as heroin and cocaine.

FACT BOX

Soft and hard drugs
*These are slang terms which distinguish between drugs which are thought to be less and more dangerous. **Hard drugs** are more powerful and potentially damaging. They are also known as 'Class A' drugs, and include heroin, cocaine and ecstasy. **Soft drugs** are considered to be less threatening and include cannabis.*

Other illegal drugs have also been thought of as addictive, and harmful, including the hallucinogenic drugs like ecstasy, LSD, cannabis and magic mushrooms. Illegal drugs (like anabolic steroids) used in sports are called performance-enhancing drugs.

Certainly there is considerable social concern about these drugs, and this is recognised by the fact that most of them are illegal in most countries. But many legal drugs are also potentially addictive if misused, including alcohol, nicotine and caffeine, as well as drugs which are used on prescription for some illnesses, such as cough medicines containing codeine.

Hard and soft illegal drugs, prescription drugs, alcohol and nicotine are similar because they all have the effect of changing something in the

FACT BOX

*The word **hallucinogenic** comes from the latin* allucinari *meaning 'to wander in the mind'. A hallucinogenic drug produces an illusion in the mind, which alters its perceptions and tricks it into thinking it can see things which are not actually present.*

mind of the person using them. This change is caused by the effect of the chemicals in the drug on the brain. Because of this, they are known as **psychoactive drugs** – *psycho* refers to the mind, and *active* refers to the fact that they produce a physical effect. These drugs are popular because of their effect on the brain – and this is the same reason why, if taken in excess, they are potentially dangerous. Hard drugs like heroin and cocaine are likely to be more dangerous because of the extreme effects they have on the chemistry of the brain – and also because of the way they are taken, through injection and 'sniffing'. This means – especially through injection – that they are taken more quickly into the bloodstream and have a strong and quick effect.

The effects and dangers of drugs are covered in more detail in Chapter 3.

SOFT AND HARD DRUGS: DOES ONE LEAD TO ANOTHER?

It is not clear whether all 'soft' drugs are addictive. There has been much discussion about whether cannabis is dangerous because it is addictive in itself, or whether it is dangerous because it can lead users on to try more harmful drugs like heroin.

FACT BOX

*When people move from using soft drugs to using hard drugs, this is known as **escalation** in drug use.*

We can explore the question of what causes escalation in more depth by using cannabis as an example. Sometimes it seems that people who use cannabis show evidence that they are addicted to it, and sometimes the evidence shows the opposite. It is certainly true that cannabis is widely used by young people, but that many who use it as teenagers or in their early twenties reduce their use as they get older and often stop using it altogether without experiencing any problems. This is an argument against it being seriously addictive.

It is also true that most people who use cannabis do not progress on to hard drugs. So when escalation to hard drugs *does* take place, it may not be the chemical properties of cannabis and their effect on the brain that cause it. Instead, it may be caused by other factors associated with using cannabis – for example, the fact that using it can bring you into contact with people selling hard drugs, and people you are with may start to use these drugs, making it easier to follow their example. This is why drug dealing is considered such a serious offence

FACT BOX

Facts about cannabis use

■ 3 million people used cannabis in the UK last year. Half of these were aged between 16 and 24.

■ 27% of young people between 16 and 24 used cannabis at least once last year. 17% of the same age group used it at least monthly.

■ There are relatively few people over 25 who use cannabis: most users are young people.

Source: Druglink Guide to Drugs – Drugscope, 2004

– because drug dealers threaten the welfare of others who they introduce to hard drugs.

Let us consider an example of someone who escalated from using soft drugs to using hard drugs.

CASE STUDY

Jane started to take cannabis when she was 13. During the next three years, she tried ecstasy, and then cocaine. She started taking heroin when she was 16. She is now 18 and dependent on it. Since she was 15, when she left home, Jane has hung out with a small circle of friends who are mainly older than she is and who all use drugs. When the group got into trouble with the law for drug dealing,

Jane's boyfriend was imprisoned and she asked for help for her addiction from a drug action team.

Jane's drug use escalated from soft to hard drugs quickly during her early teens. She developed a worrying habit, and her use of hard drugs is seriously affecting the chemistry of her brain. Heroin and cocaine are both powerfully addictive drugs. Their effects will be investigated in more detail in Chapter 3.

Alongside taking these drugs, Jane is clearly spending her time with people who are not likely to help her. As her companions are older than her and also using hard drugs, she is exposed to a way of life where using hard drugs seems normal. Jane's social circumstances are contributing to her drug problem and have caused it to escalate.

We do not know much about Jane's childhood or family background. She has left home and dropped out of school. There doesn't seem to have been anyone really trying to help her in her early teens, and it is likely that there have been difficulties at home. (We will look in detail at family difficulties that can lead to addiction in Chapter 7.)

Jane's motives for her drug use and her susceptibility to addiction can be found in the combination of:
- Difficulties at home
- *plus* lacking supportive people who try to help her
- *plus* the feelings she has about all this
- *plus* the choices she makes about who she spends time with
- *plus* the kinds of drugs she takes.

Addiction is always a complex mixture of personal, emotional and physical aspects.

It is a good sign that Jane looked for help when her boyfriend was imprisoned. As she has a habit of using hard drugs, she needs help from a professional source. This will provide her with a range of methods which aim to help with the physical and psychological aspects of her dependency. Hopefully this will also lead to her recovering from the addiction and making better lifestyle choices. Find out more about what happened to Jane in Chapter 8.

TRYING TO SOLVE EMOTIONAL PROBLEMS THROUGH TAKING DRUGS

As Jane's case study shows, drug use can often come about through a complicated mix of reasons. It is not simply a case of drug use escalating – we have to look at the reasons people started using drugs in the first place. Drugs can seem to offer a short cut to feeling good, and a way of diverting misery and bad feelings. It is easy to see how they seem attractive and tempting: it is a fact of human nature that we often feel we need a way out from our emotions. With drugs, the troubles of the world and the angst of our life can be reduced and forgotten – *for a time*.

CASE STUDY

The former Chelsea footballer, Adrian Mutu, described taking drugs to try to solve emotional problems. Talking to BBC's Football Focus *he said: 'I got drunk, very easily because I don't usually drink, and I took cocaine. It was a mistake. I didn't want to be sad and lonely. I wanted to be happy and I took it…' Find out below how Mutu is dealing with his drug use.*

Mutu is one of many examples of famous people who use drugs – some of these are celebrities, musicians, radical thinkers, athletes, politicians, barristers and civil servants. Sometimes their use is more successfully regulated; for others, like Mutu, it gets out of control.

But as we have seen, depending on an addiction to solve your problems rather than using real people around you for support is never a good idea.

CASE STUDY

The footballer Adrian Mutu is currently undergoing treatment at the Sporting Chance clinic. He says that the therapy he has received has helped him to understand more about his life and about how to change it, and he advises that 'when you are sad and lonely you have to ask for help, to speak to people who can help you'.

Freud and drugs

Sigmund Freud was the founder of psychoanalysis, which is a method of treating mental problems by recognising the importance of unconscious fears and conflicts. Freud thought that drugs could be used to help us forget our woes – but that they were dangerous because they deny us the ability to use our capacities for thinking about our experiences. By 'drowning our sorrows' we also destroy our ability to understand and make sense of our experiences. He said:

'With the help of this "drowner of cares" one can at any time withdraw from the pressures of reality and find refuge in a world of one's own with better conditions of sensibility … It is precisely the property of intoxicants which also determines their danger and their injuriousness.'

Modern psychoanalysts, like Christopher Bollas, also think that drugs block off the part of the mind that gives us the opportunity to learn emotionally from the experiences we have.

CASE STUDY

Ahmed, 16, was very lacking in self-confidence in social situations. He was terribly anxious when with his peers and particularly when talking to girls. Although his family was Muslim and was strictly against drinking alcohol, Ahmed started to drink before meeting his friends and he found that he felt much more confident. His parents were furious with him when they found out he was drinking and threatened to disown him, but Ahmed's drinking escalated so much that he would spend many nights drunk each week, and he frequently became involved in fights in pubs and clubs.

Ahmed's use of alcohol seemed to give his confidence a boost. This is because, taken in small doses, alcohol provides a temporary sense of relaxation and well-being. However, when Ahmed continued to use alcohol he developed aggressive and violent behaviour. Alcohol can lead to aggressive behaviour because it **disinhibits** a person, meaning that it reduces the constraints and limitations that we normally feel in social circumstances. In other words, it means that we take less notice of what we think other people might think of us. Mostly these constraints are extremely important, so that we do not act on all our impulses. But for people like Ahmed, too much inhibition caused by great anxiety in social circumstances is extremely frustrating. So Ahmed's drug use was a response to an emotional problem he had.

Disinhibition

Otto Fenichel, a psychoanalyst, made the ironic observation that

'the superego is soluble in alcohol'.

The superego is the name for the way we organise our conscience, our moral codes, and our ideals. It helps us decide what we should do, and what we should refrain from doing. Sometimes it seems that the superego criticises us all the time, making us anxious about not living up to the standards it sets us – or, at times, making us want to break free of the constraints it places upon us. 'Dissolving' the superego in alcohol – i.e. getting drunk and losing your inhibitions – is a way of getting temporary relief from these criticisms.

The disinhibiting effect of alcohol is examined in more depth in the next chapter.

The emotional reasons for taking drugs to excess often lie beneath the surface. This means that we may not know directly why we take a particular drug or get involved in a specific addictive activity. Or we may know what we feel, but think this is not bearable. The emotional contribution to getting harmed by drug use is often quite complex and subtle. But we do know that emotional difficulties contribute to the choice to take drugs and increase the risk of taking them to excess.

SUMMARY

In this chapter we have explored some of the social and personal causes of drug taking in young people and seen how these can lead to addiction to hard drugs. We have seen how drugs can be used to try to overcome life difficulties and that, when used addictively, in excess and regularly, some serious consequences can ensue. You can find out more about the social and emotional causes of addiction in Chapter 7. We have seen how the individuals in the case studies chose different drugs to try to deal with the different problems they were experiencing. In the next chapter we will focus on the effects of different drugs on the brain so that we can understand why, for example, Ahmed turned to alcohol rather than LSD. After this we will look at some important coping strategies.

THE EFFECTS OF DRUG USE
How do drugs affect the brain? Why do some people have bad experiences?

In the previous chapter we saw how emotional factors and life experiences can lead to drug use which then escalates to addiction. In this chapter we will look in more detail at the effects of drug use.

HOW DRUGS AFFECT THE BRAIN

Addiction and other effects of drug use come about through the *action* of the drug on the chemistry of the brain. We therefore need to understand how drugs produce these different effects – to see how they create changes in our body and mind.

Drugs affect us both in ways we can notice and in ways we can't. For example, you will notice that if you take an aspirin because you have a headache, the pain of your headache (usually) lessens. Or if you take amphetamine, you will notice that it increases your heart rate and reduces your appetite. So the effects of drugs can be studied through observing noticeable changes they cause in the person.

But these noticeable effects have themselves been caused by changes which are not immediately noticeable – changes which have been caused by the drug altering the chemistry of the brain. Different psychoactive drugs affect the chemistry of the brain in different ways, reacting with different chemicals in the brain. Some act more quickly than others and the effects of some last for longer than others. The chemicals in the drug either:

1 Increase the work of some chemical systems in the brain

or

2 Reduce the functioning of some chemical systems by dampening them down.

So: all drugs disturb the *balance* of the brain's chemistry.

The chemistry of the brain

The **Central Nervous System** (the brain and spinal column) consists of about 180 billion nerve cells, called **neurons**. These are the point of contact in the brain for drugs. They have the function of processing and storing all kinds of information to coordinate all the functions of the brain (movement, sensory perception, intellect and language, memory, feelings). They communicate with each other by releasing chemical substances which form **neurotransmitter systems**.

There are five main neurotransmitter systems. The parts of these that are most important in analysing the action of drugs are:
- **Adenosine** – has the effect of keeping us calm. It dampens down activity
- **Acetylochine** – has the effect of focusing alertness
- **Serotonin** – is responsible for generating a sense of pleasure and well-being
- **Dopamine** – increases activity and energy

- **Endorphins** – reduce feelings of pain
- **GABA** (gamma-aminobutyric acid) – a control mechanism which prevents other parts of the system from over-stimulating.

Taking drugs 'hijacks' these crucial mechanisms in the brain whose purpose is to contribute to health and well-being, and whose functioning has evolved over time in response to the need to adapt to the environment.

The process by which a drug acts on the brain can be summarised like this:

1. When a drug is taken, it is absorbed into the bloodstream. It travels towards the brain cells which react to the chemicals in the drug.

2. The drug 'homes in' on parts of the brain (surface of brain cells) which are receptive to it.

3. The action of the drug raises or lowers the level of chemical activity in some brain cells.

4. This makes you feel different in particular ways – for example, in the way you move, perceive things, remember, speak, think and feel.

When a drug has been taken persistently, the brain's chemistry adapts to its presence and treats it as though it is part of the brain's own system, so that when it is removed, the need to repeat the drug intake is felt. This explains the feelings of physical withdrawal and craving. Persistent use of a drug changes the chemistry of the brain.

HOW DIFFERENT DRUGS WORK ON THE BRAIN

It is important to know how different commonly used drugs affect the brain. Increasingly, neuroscience is able to identify which drugs affect which parts of the brain and in which ways. This is how we understand the effects of drugs on the brain and consequently how they change our behaviour. We can also understand how the chemicals of a drug affect the individual in the short term and the longer term.

Commonly used (and misused) drugs are classified in four main categories. These are **stimulants, depressants, analgesics** (including **opiates**) and **psychedelics**. Thus the characteristics of these drug categories are shown in the box:

Categories of drugs: their properties

Stimulants – These drugs increase alertness, concentration and motivation. Drugs in this category include caffeine, nicotine, amphetamine and cocaine.

Depressants – These drugs reduce tensions, anxieties and symptoms such as not being able to get to sleep. Drugs in this category include alcohol and tranquillisers (including benzodiazepines such as Valium or Librium, often known as 'jellies').

Analgesics (opiates) – These drugs reduce pain. They include heroin, morphine, methadone and codeine.

Psychedelics – This is a broad category of drugs which cause an altered consciousness and dream-like states. They include ecstasy, LSD, magic mushrooms, mescaline and cannabis.

Let us now look at some of the commonly used drugs in these categories, arranged here in alphabetical order.

Alcohol

Alcohol is a depressant – it has the effect of shutting down many of the brain's functions, including the system that controls inhibition.

Alcohol (and some other psychoactive drugs) can place us in danger through seeming to offer freedom from normal constraints. Feeling 'free from constraints' can lead us into dangerous situations like driving after drinking, or getting into fights. Sometimes, the disinhibition from drinking alcohol can lead to destructive impulses being given 'freedom' to act, and we can harm ourselves and others.

Although it is very widely used, alcohol is a highly addictive drug. Many people are able to keep their alcohol intake small – so they drink a little, not a lot. It has even been shown that a small amount of alcohol has a beneficial effect on health – but this is an amount as small as one unit per day.

Amphetamine

Amphetamine is a stimulant, and acts like cocaine (see page 37) on the systems which increase pleasure and energy.

FACT BOX

Alcohol and the brain
The disinhibiting effect of alcohol is explained by the chemical effects it has on the brain. It reacts with, and increases the activity of, a chemical in the brain whose job is to make sure that other systems do not over-function. This chemical is called **GABA** *(gamma-aminobutyric acid), and it is a very important control mechanism.*

Alcohol has the effect of reducing the overall activity of the brain. Taken in small amounts the effects are to reduce tension and anxiety, increase pleasure and reduce self-criticism and conscience. But reducing or closing down brain cell activity includes closing down those systems which monitor and prevent behaviour we would usually feel is undesirable, including violence and aggression, making them much harder to control. It also reduces our control of movements and intellect.

FACT BOX

Did you know that alcohol is the second highest cause of death by poisoning after carbon monoxide? These two agents cause more deaths by poisoning than all other poisons put together.

Excess alcohol poisons by causing swelling in the base of the brain, where the centres of respiratory and cardiovascular regulation (which control the working of the heart and lungs) are located. 'Binge' drinking can lead to alcohol poisoning.

Current concerns about binge drinking and drinking excessively and quickly are therefore soundly based, as this behaviour is potentially very dangerous.

Caffeine

Caffeine acts as a stimulant by reducing the activity of a chemical in the brain which has the effect of keeping us calm. Caffeine therefore increases alertness. So it is not a good idea to take coffee or tea (or in fact to drink cola, which also contains caffeine) immediately before you want to go to sleep.

Cannabis

Cannabis is a psychedelic, and its effects include creating feelings of relaxation, talkativeness and hilarity, causing hallucinations and making you feel hungry or tired. It can also cause distress and paranoia. (The different effects of cannabis are examined in more detail in the section 'good' trips and 'bad' trips, later in this chapter.)

FACT BOX

What is a hallucinogenic drug?

Hallucinogenic drugs like **ecstasy, LSD** and **cannabis** affect the part of the brain which provides feelings of satisfaction and well-being. However, just how the hallucinogenic effects come about is not really known. One view is that the drugs dampen down visual perceptions and awareness of time, leading to the distortions of visual and time perception.

Risks from taking these drugs include not being able to respond appropriately to realities.

CAN CANNABIS MAKE YOU GO MAD?

For some people, cannabis can trigger quite frightening feelings of unreality. Sometimes, the effects can include delusions – for example, altering your perception of how far you are from the ground. In some cases people have leapt out of buildings or off bridges, because they have had a delusion that they can fly or not be hurt by doing something dangerous. So, by altering your perceptions, cannabis can make you do things that seem mad.

In addition, some young people can seem to get symptoms of mental illness through taking cannabis and other drugs. Usually, this happens because there are difficulties anyway. Drug taking doesn't usually cause mental illness but it can be very frightening when underlying emotions and conflicts come to the surface in this way. Sometimes having emotional difficulties leads to drug misuse; and using drugs makes these emotional difficulties worse. The combination of emotional difficulties and drug misuse is usually called **dual diagnosis**.

FACT BOX

Dual diagnosis
Having both emotional (mental health) difficulties and problems with drug misuse is now referred to as 'dual diagnosis'. Drug use can worsen the difficulties experienced by someone with emotional or psychological problems and these difficulties can sometimes increase the psychoactive effects of the drugs.

CASE STUDY

Simon had a great deal of difficulty with his temper as a child and in his early teens. He started to take cannabis with his friends when he was 15. He began to take it in increasing quantities, as he initially

*liked the sense of relaxation it gave him. However, he started to get
some very disturbing effects afterwards which frightened him.
Particularly worrying for him was a sense of almost complete
numbness and a lack of reality, so that he could not know for sure if
the world was real. Simon really felt he had gone mad. He talked to
his parents who arranged for him to have a meeting with a
psychotherapist.*

*It is a good sign that Simon is able to talk to his parents and that they
arrange for him to see a psychotherapist. This will make it possible for
him to explore, in a safe setting with a sympathetic professional, how
his emotional difficulties might be affecting him. He seems to have a
problem with aggressive feelings, and it might seem that cannabis
would be helpful for people who have difficulties with anger and
rage. But in fact, the effect of taking drugs only makes these feelings
less accessible, it does not take them away. And Simon's emotional
difficulties may have led to his 'bad' response to cannabis. When
taking soft drugs brings about his kind of emotional reaction it is wise
to stay clear of all drugs. But when you are faced with an emotional
difficulty, the temptation to ease the pain by taking something can be
powerful.*

Cocaine

Cocaine is a stimulant which powerfully increases the activity of
systems in the brain which influence levels of pleasure and energy. Its
effects include:

- A sense of pleasure, satisfaction and well-being
- Increased energy and reduced inhibitions
- Feelings of exhilaration and the ability to ignore pain and tiredness
- Feelings of having great physical strength and mental power.

Cocaine creates an illusion that there are no limits to what you can achieve and denies the ordinary need for rest. As you become addicted to cocaine, you need to use it repeatedly in order to avoid feeling down – and ordinary.

Heroin

Heroin is often thought of as being one of the most dangerous drugs. It is formed from the opium poppy and is therefore called an **opiate**. Opiates influence a very wide range of brain functions, and their effects include:

▨ Pain reduction (**analgesia**). Heroin and other opiates activate **endorphins**, the purpose of which is to reduce pain. A similar effect is achieved by prolonged exercise which also releases endorphins
▨ Changes to appetite, learning and memory
▨ Changes to the parts of the brain which are responsible for pleasurable feelings.

Heroin users sometimes talk of the effect as being very comforting, like 'being wrapped up in a duvet'. The destructiveness of heroin is that it provides a blanket which is not real – although it feels like it is comforting the body, in reality it is harming it and killing it.

Nicotine

Nicotine is classed as a stimulant. It is an extremely addictive substance – 30 per cent of those who try smoking once become addicts! As is well known, smoking carries high risk of causing serious illness and death. Nicotine increases the activity of a system in the brain which heightens attention and alertness. Smoking cigarettes heightens alertness rather than, as some advertisements for nicotine suggest, having a calming effect on you. Famously, the advert for the

Hamlet cigar shows the smoker achieving calm by lighting up in a chaotic scene where everything that could go wrong has done. But it is not a function of nicotine to create calm – the calming effects come from satisfying the addiction to cigarettes! The habit of smoking cigarettes sets up a pattern in which frustration is satisfied by smoking. Any frustrations someone feels can be channelled into wanting a cigarette!

See the resources section for organisations that can tell you more about how drugs work.

'GOOD' TRIPS AND 'BAD' TRIPS

People who take a drug can experience different effects at different times. This is especially true of cannabis and some hallucinogenic drugs like ecstasy and LSD. With LSD the concepts of a 'good trip' and a 'bad trip' have emerged from the varied experiences reported by different people using the same drug. The effects of taking drugs depends on:

- The chemistry of the body and the drug
- The user's mood or state of mind at the time of taking the drug
- The setting in which the drug is taken.

Cannabis provides a very good example of this. The effects of taking it tend to produce a range of pleasant and unpleasant experiences:

- Pleasant effects include relaxation, talkativeness and hilarity
- Hallucinogenic effects include confusion of thought processes, forgetfulness and the feeling that time is passing more quickly or slowly

- Unpleasant effects include anxiety, distress, panic and paranoia
- Other effects include feeling hungry and tired.

Pleasant effects (or 'good trips') are more easily obtained by experienced users taking the drug in a relaxed setting with friends. Some users are more likely to experience the hallucinogenic effects, and some may be more prone to the unpleasant effects (or 'bad trips'), especially if they have underlying emotional problems.

SUMMARY

With all this in mind, it is now possible to explain why Ahmed and Jane, whose experiences we looked at in Chapter 2, and Simon, who we have looked at in this chapter, chose the drugs they did. All of them felt unable to draw on resources from inside themselves to address the emotional difficulties they had. So they turned to drugs instead. Trying to boost his lack of self-confidence, Ahmed turned to alcohol so that he could use the effects of reducing inhibitions that alcohol provides. Jane's combination of drugs (or **polydrug use**) aimed to dampen down painful feelings (heroin) and provide energy (cocaine). And Simon took cannabis to relieve the difficulty he had with aggressive feelings – but in fact, these aggressive feelings only led to him having bad experiences with the drug he chose.

THE ADDICTIVE AND DANGEROUS PROPERTIES OF PSYCHOACTIVE DRUGS

As mentioned at the beginning of Chapter 2, taking drugs is not *always* dangerous and does not *always* result in addiction. Drugs become dangerous and addictive in ways listed below. Ask yourself if you are putting yourself at risk from any of the following nine points.

1 **Taking too much**. There is a danger of physical ill health and in extreme circumstances of death from taking an excessive amount of some psychoactive drugs. Opiates and alcohol pose particular dangers from overdoses.

2 **Taking powerful drugs in dangerous ways**. Class A drugs are in Class A because they have very powerful effects and can be taken in ways (e.g. injected) which maximise the way they affect the body. Injection also carries the risk of infection from contaminated needles (although there are services for ensuring the safe exchange of needles).

3 **Endangering your physical health through persistent use**. The risks of tobacco and alcohol are high from persistent use. It is widely known now that tobacco leads to premature death through lung cancer and coronary diseases. Persistent and excessive alcohol use leads to a variety of potentially fatal conditions. These include heart disease, disease of the respiratory (breathing) system, and damage to the liver.

Drug related deaths (in England and Wales)

	Drug related deaths 1996-2001	Approximate numbers of users
Cocaine	338	600,000
Amphetamine	390	500,000
Ecstasy	161	700,000
Heroin/Morphine	4126	60,000
Methadone	1896	40,000
Alcohol	200,000 –400,000 (approx)	millions

Source: Office for National Statistics

4 **Endangering your mental health through persistent use**.
Psychoactive drugs have a deep effect on the functioning of the
brain and can change the way it works. This can mean that your
own resources for creating comfort and energy are bypassed, and
because they are not used, they fade away. Heroin sets up an
endless, unstoppable craving once the initial pleasurable state
fades. Nicotine also seems to demand repeated usage. (Other
psychoactive drugs have less addictive qualities. For example, we
have seen that the addictive quality of cannabis has been the
subject of much debate and there is still no clear evidence that
physical addiction results from cannabis use.)

5 **Taking drugs in combinations**. Some combinations of drug are
particularly dangerous. Combining alcohol with some tranquillisers
comes into this category. Some users take combinations of drugs
for their combined effects – for example, heroin is used to provide
a sense of comfort, and cocaine to provide energy.

6 **Losing your sense of reality**. Dangers can occur whilst taking
some drugs because there is a changed relationship with external
reality. For example, as we have seen, hallucinogenic drugs distort
your experience of space and time.

7 **Believing that you are 'safe' because you are using legal
drugs**. *Remember that illegal drugs are not necessarily more
dangerous than legal drugs*. There is a fine line to be drawn
between legal and illegal drugs in terms of dangerousness. Alcohol
is strongly addictive and causes considerable harm through illness
and alcohol-related accidents. Tobacco is amongst the most
addictive substances known.

8 **Believing the illusion that drugs make you feel better**. Most
psychoactive drugs provide anyone taking them with an initial
'positive' effect, in terms of generating a feeling of greater well-
being, satisfaction, calm or heightened attention and energy. This

is followed, however, by a significant negative, undesirable and potentially harmful effect. Harmful effects can be either physical or psychological, or both. Some drugs, such as alcohol and heroin, generate both physical and psychological dependency.

9 **The increased effects on you if you have emotional problems**. If you have emotional or psychological difficulties you are more likely to be vulnerable to the effects of drugs and less able to control use and effects. Sometimes the effects of the drugs can be heightened.

COPING WITH USING DRUGS

In the last two chapters we have seen some of the causes of drug use as well as some of the effects. The points above should have helped you decide whether or not you have (or are likely to develop) a problem with drug use. Now it is time to look at ways of coping with drug use. There are some important coping strategies for using psychoactive drugs of all kinds.

1 If you decide you want to take drugs, be sure of your motivation for doing so. Trying to solve your problems is not a good reason for taking drugs. You will only get new problems to add to the old ones! You will also weaken your own capacities and resources through not using them and relying on the drugs instead.

2 If you do take drugs, take them in a safe setting – don't risk harming yourself whilst under the influence. This includes driving, fighting with others and acting on delusions. It is only through being with others who are not similarly affected by drugs and who have your interests at heart that you can be in a 'safe' setting – they will realise if, for example, you are having a delusion which may cause you to do something dangerous.

3 | Think carefully about the company you keep – are your friends and companions interested in their health and well-being, and in yours? If not, think about changing your friends.

4 | Choose drugs carefully – make sure you can regulate your use of them. If you are at risk of taking them excessively, **stop**.

5 | If you have a bad experience taking a drug, take it seriously – you might have got in touch with an emotional difficulty you have and you should talk this over with others.

6 | Avoid hard drugs – always.

7 | If you are taking hard drugs, get professional help – now.

8 | If you use drugs and don't think you have a problem, try stopping. What does it feel like? If you are missing the drugs, or feel preoccupied with taking them, you have a problem – get some help from people you trust.

9 | When you are not taking drugs is the best time to make an accurate assessment of your need for them, but you must be honest with yourself. Take account of what people you trust say about you: drug taking is a source of self-deceit. If you find you don't want to take any notice of others' views and feel other people don't know you like you do yourself, think of the self-deceit in the saying: 'Giving up is easy – I've done it a thousand times'. Does this fit you?

Remember that turning to drugs rather than people for support is never a good idea. For more information on how to get support from other people, and on how to get out of addictions, go to Chapter 8.

CHAPTER FOUR:

GAMBLING
Why do gamblers get hooked? What goes through a gambler's mind?

Gambling is an addictive activity in which the physical, or chemical, side of things plays only a minor part. It shows that **psychological dependence** is a very important aspect of addiction.

GAMBLING IN CONTEXT

Gambling is a widely practised activity, and one which has become increasingly legalised in the past twenty years. There is currently a debate about the legalisation of large scale casinos, Vegas style, in Britain. This has generated a lot of debate about whether gambling is a 'harmless' and enjoyable pastime, or whether it has some serious social and individual consequences.

You will probably have had some contact with gambling through family involvement in the lottery and scratch cards and the legal slot or fruit machine arcades in most towns and cities in the UK. Playing fruit machines is a very popular activity for teenagers. It has been estimated that 65 per cent of the population play the fruit machines at some point, and between 5 and 10 per cent are regular players, which means playing at least once a week.

FACT BOX

Did you know that fruit machine arcades are legal for under 18s in the UK, but this is not the case in the USA and most European countries?

Of course, occasional gambling is not really a serious issue, especially for low stakes. In the same way that a glass of wine or beer can enhance an enjoyable social event, some families enjoy gambling, not necessarily expecting to win the lottery each week, but enjoying the excitement of the possibility of winning. Being able to bear the disappointment of losing, having a realistic attitude towards how much should be wagered, and not getting emotionally reliant on success are necessary for gambling to remain a 'social' rather than an addictive experience.

Occasional gambling has to be separated from more serious involvement. Two categories have been widely used to identify more addictive, dangerous gambling behaviour:

Pathological gambling is the most serious and this is characterised by:
- Continuous or periodic loss of control over gambling
- An obsession or preoccupation with gambling
- A preoccupation with obtaining money to gamble with
- Irrational thinking about gambling
- Continuing with the behaviour despite adverse consequences.

Problem gambling is a term which has been used to define gambling where the person shows some – but not all – of the above characteristics. Typically, they would be less heavily involved and have more control. Nevertheless, they might also show signs of moving towards more pathological gambling or, alternatively, towards becoming less involved.

Most estimates, across a number of countries, show that pathological gambling affects between 1 per cent and 2 per cent of the population.

You might notice that the criteria for pathological gambling are similar to criteria for addiction. It can 'take over' and become the most important thing in your life.

Gambling takes over

A French writer, Jean Barbeyrac, wrote a three-volume work on gambling which was published in 1737. In it, he describes gambling as an intense passion, which is an enemy from which there is no escape. Gambling seems to be completely overwhelming, as it never lets you out of its grip for a moment. He wrote:

'The more one plays the more one wishes to play … it seems that gambling had acquired the right to occupy all the gambler's thoughts.'

The person's mood becomes more pleasurable when engaged in the activity and an unpleasant feeling occurs when it is suddenly stopped. The gambler has a confused state of mind about her/his gambling – but continues despite the problems it may be causing. It starts to take more intense and frequent involvement to obtain pleasure (in other words the gambler becomes 'tolerant') and, after giving up, the person is subject to relapses.

GETTING HOOKED ON GAMBLING

As with psychoactive drugs, becoming intensely involved with gambling is a process. Initially the idea of winning some money might be the motive and the pleasure in taking part in gambling can actually be quite intense. It has been suggested that the intensity of excitement brought about by gambling can be a major factor in taking it up. The pleasure of this excitement may be more important than any realistic hope of making money. The initial attractions of gambling can include a sense of escaping from unhappy, miserable feelings and experiencing surges of emotion.

It has been suggested that gambling can lead to changes in the chemistry of the brain, and therefore have a similar effect to taking drugs. These changes include dampening down of pain (endorphin release) and pleasurable energy (dopamine system). (The effect of drugs on the chemistry of the brain is explained in more detail in Chapter 3.) Gamblers sometimes describe the effects of gambling as like sexual excitement. Winning is a 'high' and losing a 'downer'.

The excitement of the gambling hall

The Russian novelist Fyodor Dostoevsky is an example of a famous person who was a compulsive gambler. He wrote an autobiographical novel, *The Gambler*, which conveys the excitement of the gambling hall. He wrote: 'As soon as I begin to hear the chinking of money being poured out I almost go into convulsions'. His gambling was so intense that he lied to his wife and pawned jewellery to get money to gamble with.

'...pleasure and excitement begin to exist alongside unpleasant feelings.'

It is probably useful to think of a 'gambling escalator', in which the addiction progressively gets hold of you.

- Firstly, there is an initial attraction and excitement. There follows a stage in the gambling escalator where pleasure and excitement begin to exist alongside unpleasant feelings when the person is not gambling. The unpleasant feelings are similar to withdrawal effects.

- Further up the escalator, gamblers start to try to play more often, and to do this may obtain money from all sources. Additionally, gambling becomes used as a means of paying debts and 'chasing losses', which means that the gambler attempts to recover losses through further gambling. Stakes rise. The gambler's relationships are affected by the attempts to keep the extent of the gambling secret which can involve them in deceit.

- At the top of the escalator, the gambler gets caught in a vicious circle: their method of dealing with their problem is to try to obtain money and recoup losses through more gambling whilst keeping their gambling a secret, especially within close relationships. This leads to negative feelings (such as depression, guilt, anger, anxiety and desperation) and these feelings are relieved only through further gambling.

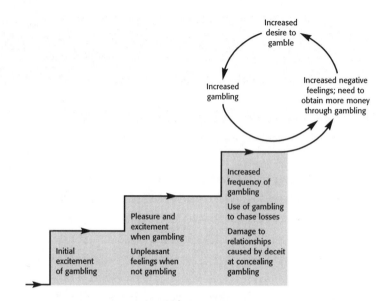

CASE STUDY

Martin was a promising and successful athlete until he had an accident when he was 16 which seriously threatened his career. When he was recovering from his accident he started to play the fruit machines. He got hooked and he used every trick he could think of to get money to use on the machines. He did not enjoy anything when he wasn't playing the machines. He began to go to casinos and he developed an obsession about going to Las Vegas. He said that he felt the same things when gambling as he had done before an athletics meeting – an intense excitement, nervousness and anticipation. He knew he could lose, but if he won he had the chance of feeling 'absolutely brilliant'. Martin's case shows clearly how gambling can be used as an attempt to overcome disappointments and 'ordinary' feelings: through his conviction that a 'brilliant' feeling could be obtained, Martin hoped he would be able to forget about the ordinary pains and realities of life. He got so involved in the fruit machines that he started to miss school and eventually failed his exams. Then he got into arguments with his parents who had not pushed him earlier because of his accident. Reluctantly, he took his parents' advice and went for some help from a counsellor.

HOW GAMBLERS THINK

Another feature of pathological gamblers is the way that they experience a false sense of mastery and control when playing. Rather than feeling at the mercy of the machine, ticket or game, the gambler develops a false set of beliefs and thoughts about:

- How to beat the system
- Skill playing a big part (when in reality it is down to luck)
- Believing that you can 'know the sequences'.

Having a win provokes the belief that 'luck has turned' and this reinforces the desire to keep playing. Some people playing fruit machines even personalise them, thinking that a particular machine 'likes' him or that they have a way of knowing what goes on inside the machine. Gamblers also get addicted to throwing it all away. But by being addicted, your skills, talents and capacities are also thrown away.

'Gamblers get addicted to throwing it all away.'

These irrational thoughts seem very important in understanding how gambling can become a way of pushing aside miserable feelings and experiences in relationships and how the gambler cannot face the true randomness of the fruit machine, lottery ticket or spin of the roulette wheel.

The vicious circle of gambling – as for every addiction – means that keeping the gambling going becomes the most important thing. This means that everything is geared towards getting the money to gamble with and being ruthless about this.

The psychologist Mark Griffiths has studied young people who were addicted to the fruit machines. He talked with them about how they started playing, and how they felt about their addiction. They all thought they started when they were 11 and were addicted between 13 and 15. They said they were always trying to borrow money to play with. All of them said they felt bad about their lives but nevertheless continued to play. One boy said he had spent money given to him for Christmas on Christmas day morning. They said they hated the fruit machines, describing them as 'deadly' and 'life destroyers', and saying that 'they should be banned'.

Martin, whose experiences were described earlier in this chapter, was also very single-minded in his obsession with gambling. Unlike the people in Mark Griffiths's study, Martin's parents were successful in getting him to seek help from a counsellor. Being able to communicate his feelings and motives about gambling helped him to put his gambling behaviour – and state of mind – into perspective and value other parts of his life more.

COPING WITH GAMBLING

Some of the coping mechanisms you need to avoid getting caught up in a gambling addiction are similar to those needed with drug taking. First you need to assess where you are in relation to gambling. Try answering the following questions:

1. Do you spend a lot of time gambling?

[2] If you do, do you think about it when you are not playing?

[3] If you honestly assess your gambling activity, is it progressing to higher amounts and greater frequency?

[4] Do you borrow, beg or steal money to use on gambling?

[5] Do you lie to others about what the money is for?

[6] Have you ruined your chances in something important (especially at school or at work, or in relationships with others) through gambling?

[7] Do you keep playing even if you feel bad about it?

If you answered 'yes' to some or all of the above questions you should really try to stop gambling, and seek advice and help. Martin was helped by his parents, and there may be people you trust who you can turn to. Don't be afraid to seek help – like counselling – if you are in difficulties like this.

You can also assess the following for yourself:

[1] Check out the company you keep: is gambling high priority for the group you are in?

[2] Are you (like Martin) trying not to face a loss or disappointment you have had in your life by recreating the excitement/interest through gambling?

If you answer 'yes' to either of these two questions you should think about changing your friendship group and facing up to aspects of your life you may be trying to avoid. It would be helpful to talk things through with an adult you trust and to consider approaching a service providing counselling or psychotherapy.

For more information on how to seek help, see Chapter 8.

CHAPTER FIVE:

EATING DISORDERS
What is an eating disorder and how does it develop?

People can get addicted to eating, dieting, exercising and sex. It seems odd that these things, which are so essential for life and health, can get turned into addictions. But every aspect of our lives that involves powerful feelings *can* be turned into an addiction. Other examples are shopping and watching TV. Some people develop patterns of eating, exercising and sexual behaviour that are addictive and that threaten their physical and mental well-being. These addictive patterns often begin in the teenage years.

In order to understand these problems better, we need to see how they develop and how they might become addictive. In this chapter the focus will be on eating disorders. The next chapter will be about exercise, sex, and the internet.

WHAT IS AN EATING DISORDER?

An **eating disorder** is the name given to a serious problem with eating. These problems include being extremely underweight – or, at the other extreme, being very overweight. The main conditions are:

Anorexia nervosa (also referred to as **restrictive anorexia**): in this disorder, the person diets too much, and maintains a very low body weight by avoiding eating fattening food to restrict the intake of calories. Alongside this there is usually an obsession with exercise, and use of certain drugs (for example laxatives and diuretics) to keep body weight down.

Bulimia nervosa: in this disorder, a preoccupation with and craving for food leads to bouts of excessive eating, known as 'bingeing'. This is followed by vomiting – which is usually self-induced, and taking purgatives and diuretics. The aim is both to satisfy the craving for food *and* to keep your weight down.

Binge eating: in this disorder, as in bulimia, there is a craving for food, which leads to binge eating. But instead of controlling the weight gain which follows from the binges (by vomiting, etc.) there is no

FACT BOX

Laxative comes from the Latin word laxare meaning 'to loosen'. (It is linked to our English word relax.) When you take a laxative, it loosens your bowels – meaning that whatever you eat is processed and comes out very quickly at the other end! Laxatives are also referred to as purgatives. *Diuretics have a similar effect to laxatives – but instead of making you process food quickly, they make you process liquid quickly.*

attempt to compensate and you become overweight. The state of being very overweight is called **obesity**.

CASE STUDIES

The following three case studies illustrate the main kinds of eating disorders.

__Francesca__, who is now 21, has been a restrictive anorexic since she was 15. She weighs 40 kilos, and is 1.67 metres tall, so her BMI (see page 61) is 14.3 – so she must be considered to be seriously underweight. She thinks about food all the time, and writes all these thoughts in a diary. She eats very little and exercises excessively, cycling for hours and spending lunchtime swimming lengths in the pool rather than eating. If she can't exercise she gets upset and agitated.

__Peter__ is bulimic. He began at 15 by bingeing on food from the fridge, especially ice cream. When he started to binge he would eat without being able to stop and afterwards he vomited. He was worried about becoming overweight and he thought that if this happened he would not be popular with his friends. He thought that bingeing and vomiting was the 'ideal' solution because he could satisfy his craving for food and stay popular with his friends. His weight fluctuated quite dramatically.

__Sharon__, now in her early 20s, started to get overweight when she was in her late teens. She is now so overweight that she has difficulty moving around. When she talks, she seems to be unaffected by her problems, and there is seemingly no trace of pain, depression or unhappiness. She snacks continually, saying she cannot do without this.

Later in this chapter we will look at how Francesca, Peter and Sharon were able to deal with their problems.

HOW DO EATING DISORDERS DEVELOP?

The reasons people might develop an eating disorder are both social and psychological. There are extremely powerful social pressures (especially on young women) to develop and maintain a very thin body. Although the majority of people with eating disorders are female, ten per cent are male. Many of the personalities in movies, fashion and the pop world have this 'idealised' thin body – for example Naomi Campbell and Victoria Beckham. There is some evidence that the media can affect how we think about ourselves, our perceptions and expectations of ourselves and our bodies.

FACT BOX

The media can change our ideals

In Fiji, after TV programmes from the USA were introduced, girls and young women became dissatisfied with the way they looked and wanted to look more like characters in the programmes they had watched. Eighty-three per cent of Fijian women thought that TV had influenced their perceptions of body image and size.

It would be wrong to think that eating disorders are simply a modern problem, as there are many examples from people in history.

FACT BOX

Self-starvation in history
In the middle ages a nun, Catherine of Siena, starved herself in the course of her religious devotions. She described becoming quite ecstatic when she had deprived herself of food.

Self-starvation (or 'hunger striking') was used as a political weapon by, amongst others, the suffragettes, Gandhi and the Irish Republican hunger strikers.

The fact that self-starvation has been used as a political protest makes us think that modern anorexia might be a protest against something too. Perhaps people with eating disorders are protesting against someone or something they feel has hurt or injured them in some way.

For example, Francesca, whose anorexia was described in the case study above, was very upset that her parents had separated when she was 13, and she felt that her mother did not understand her. Francesca was often angry with her mother.

The ways that eating disorders develop are distinctly driven by our own preoccupations and expectations. Because our society is so preoccupied with consumption of all kinds, and we are always being invited to think we really must have something we haven't got, it is difficult for us to regulate our wants and needs.

'We are likely to turn to food when we are unhappy and miserable or frustrated.'

There is also strong social pressure on us to be in control. We are meant to be disciplined at work or school and capable of letting go when we go out. It is a difficult balance to strike. Controlling our food intake – or letting it get out of control – is a way of dealing with these pressures.

We are also likely to turn to food when we are unhappy and miserable or frustrated. Often this happens when we feel that there is no one else who will love us or look after us in the way we want to be loved or looked after. We talk often of 'comfort eating', for example.

There is a current concern that we are becoming overweight, eating junk food and not taking enough exercise. At the same time the view of what is an ideal weight and size has got lower. Lower weight is associated with greater beauty in women but there is evidence that both boys and girls have perceptions that an ideal body shape is thin. Set against our expectations and ideals, we are making ourselves seem more overweight!

THE EFFECTS OF EATING DISORDERS

The first effect of an eating disorder is that your weight becomes either very low or very high. The standard way of measuring whether your weight is in the expected range for your size is to calculate your **Body Mass Index (BMI)**.

FACT BOX

Adios Barbie!

The website Adiosbarbie (www.adiosbarbie.com) is a place where features, articles and readers' comments aim to encourage a different way of thinking about the way we look. In particular, it aims to oppose the ideal of a thin body – as displayed by the Barbie doll's thin (but large breasted) shape.

One reader's comment on the website is:

'Being skinny is overrated, first of all. And second of all, the whole idea of trying to be model thin is totally superficial and dangerous. I should know. I flirted briefly with anorexia in my freshman year of high school before I realized that I was created to look the way I do, and I realized that looks are only part of me.'

Body Mass Index (BMI)

Body mass index is calculated by dividing your weight (in kilograms) by the square of your height (your height multiplied by itself), in metres.
(If you only know your weight in feet and inches and your height in stone and pounds, you will need to convert these figures into kilograms and metres before doing the BMI calculation. The easiest way to do this is to find a converter on the internet. For more information, see the Resources section.)

$$\textbf{BMI} = \frac{\text{Weight (kgms)}}{\text{Height x Height (metres)}}$$

From this figure, you can calculate which range your BMI is in.

If your BMI is:

Under 17.5	– you are seriously underweight, anorexic
17.5–20	– you are underweight
20–25	– you are normal
25–30	– you are overweight
30–35	– you are seriously overweight

Anorexia can be so extreme that it is life threatening (a Body Mass Index of 12.5 and below is life threatening). Anorexia is a serious illness which can lead to death and can also damage vital body organs. Bulimia can also severely damage your body. Electrolyte imbalance (dangerously low levels of the essential minerals) and dehydration can cause heart problems and, occasionally, sudden death due to a heart attack.

Eating large amounts and binge eating can lead to obesity and this is problematic because it increases the risk of physical ill health. When it becomes compulsive, you can feel trapped in a vicious circle in which you crave food and cannot feel full without eating excessively, rapidly or continuously. Some people have prejudiced attitudes towards 'bigger' people – and knowing this can reduce your self-esteem, which in turn makes you want to eat more to comfort yourself. Exercise may become uncomfortable and you could feel that it is humiliating and embarrassing to be seen doing it.

There are serious physical dangers from being obese. These include:
- A predisposition to diabetes and to diseases of the heart and arteries
- Reduction in fertility
- Increased risk of developing high blood pressure.

Psychological dangers of all eating disorders include:
- Hating your body
- Being depressed
- Feeling rejected by others.

The development of an eating disorder always has powerful emotional and psychological reasons and causes. The eating disorder becomes the way in which emotional difficulties are avoided. Some people are more vulnerable to the onset of an eating disorder because of personal, family and childhood experiences. We will discuss these vulnerabilities in detail in Chapter 7.

HOW PEOPLE WITH EATING DISORDERS THINK

Eating difficulties take hold on a person, and become a 'disorder' when there is a compulsion to eat – or, in the case of the dieting anorexic, to avoid eating. People with eating disorders are obsessed by food. Addiction to eating too much or too little is similar to addiction to drugs or to gambling, in that the addict thinks about their obsession all the time.

'...time is measured in terms of food and mealtimes...'

Though someone who is a restrictive anorexic aims to avoid eating, anorexics get very preoccupied with food. Food is talked about endlessly: time is measured in terms of food and mealtimes (or how long it is since you last ate); how many calories have been taken in, or would be taken in; and how the calories will be burned off. Someone who is bulimic can get very excited about the cycles of bingeing and vomiting, and alternate between feeling intensely excited and intensely guilty.

People's thoughts about their eating disorders can also be reflected in other areas of their life. For example, someone who is bulimic can show their bulimia by 'bingeing' on shopping, getting into an excited state about reading, or doing art work and producing a lot very rapidly, then throwing it away.

FACT BOX

The word bulimia *is Greek and literally means 'having the hunger to devour an ox, bull or cow'*

A restrictive anorexic's control over food can spill over into a desire to control other aspects of their life, which can adversely affect the people around them. For example they can be very restrictive and 'mean' in their relationships, strictly controlling what is taken in from them. People suffering from anorexia can exert pressure on others by getting them to worry about the effects of the excessive dieting. Sometimes sitting with an anorexic to help them eat can involve a very long ordeal, as mealtimes can last for hours though nothing is eaten.

When an eating disorder is established, it bears very little resemblance to a desire to diet a little, or to get into better shape through exercise and healthy eating. The preoccupation with the body and with food has created the addictive vicious circle, in which it seems impossible to change the pattern of eating, dieting or exercising. Instead the disorder has all the features of an addiction, including:

■ Preoccupation with the addictive activity at the expense of other aspects of your life

■ Being unable to control the activity, or change the pattern of behaviour

■ Cravings for either food or exercise (to compensate for eating)

■ Continuing with the activity despite feedback that it is causing problems to physical health, mental health and relationships

■ Using the activity in order to deal with emotional and relationship difficulties.

COPING WITH EATING DISORDERS

Work out where you are in the process. As with all addictive activities, the extent to which anyone is involved in an eating disorder is a process: there are degrees of involvement. You need to assess how you feel about the five bulleted points above. If some of them fit you, then you should seek help.

Can you really believe someone else's view of you? The hardest thing is often to accept that someone else might be right about being worried about you – so, choosing the person who is the most objective about you, ask them what they think about your eating: how worried are they about you? Try to take their advice rather than argue with it or shrug it off!

Change your eating pattern – but don't *just* change your eating pattern. Eating disorders are not only about changing your eating patterns – though this is always necessary. Remember that there is a very strong psychological aspect to eating disorders, and that this varies from person to person. So you need to look at what the eating problem means for you and the reasons for it. This means looking at difficulties you have with your feelings and relationships. Help comes from really working on these emotional and relationship issues – often in psychotherapy – and this is how Francesca, Peter and Sharon, the examples given earlier in this chapter, got help for the reasons for their difficulties. Often, the best approach is to combine a programme of dietary help for your eating pattern with help for the emotional reasons for it. Having regular help with your diet and weight helps to keep an eye on reality.

For more information on how to seek help for an addiction, see Chapter 8.

> **For a closer look at eating disorders see**
> ***Real Life Issues: Eating Disorders***

EXERCISE, SEX AND THE INTERNET
What are these addictions, and how do they affect us?

EXCESSIVE EXERCISE

The idea that exercise is good for you and that many of us don't exercise enough is very current. It is of course true. However, we have seen that excessive exercise is part of the eating disorder anorexia, and there is concern that it can form an addictive activity on its own as well. In the previous chapter we looked at how being exposed constantly to media images of thinness affects how you feel you should look. The same is true of the prominence given to sporting stars whose thin but muscular appearance makes an image of an ideal appearance we should aspire to. The image of the thin, muscular sportsman for example is also one which we see as very sexually attractive, successful and powerful.

What is excessive exercise?

The area of excessive exercise is particularly difficult, because exercise is important for physical and mental health and it is usually a very positive thing. But ordinary exercise has limits and is fun and relaxing. Excessive exercise is quite different, because the extent and motivation are quite negative and self-destructive rather than positive and self-enhancing, and because the ordinary boundaries, or limits, have been ignored and exceeded.

The addictive quality of exercise is progressive. Increasing amounts of exercise and an increasing need for it accompany each other. Runners and workers-out cannot bear to miss a session and will continue to exercise even when they are not feeling well or when they are injured. There is also a masochistic side to this form of addiction – addicts experience a kind of pleasure in passing through the pain barrier.

'Exercising and developing your muscles can seem as though it holds you together – physically and mentally.'

Like other addictions, when exercising begins to become addictive it is used to avoid problems and difficulties – especially problems in close relationships and very self-critical feelings. Exercising and developing your muscles can seem as though it holds you together – physically and mentally. When exercise seems to be the answer to your problems, it becomes impossible not to exercise: the amount of exercise increases and you start to risk physical injury. The most common forms of excessive exercising are running and working out. Both of these provide a physical 'high' which an increasing amount of exercise is needed to maintain.

What are the criteria for addiction to exercise?

The warning signs that exercise is becoming an addiction are:

■ Feeling like exercise is a compulsion, rather than fun

- Feeling guilty, depressed or irritable when you don't exercise
- Feeling like your job, studies or relationships get in the way of exercise
- Missing school, college or work in order to exercise
- Exercising regardless of injuries, tiredness or illness
- Ignoring the concerns of your friends and family about your attitude to exercise.

What are the causes and effects of excessive exercise?

Excessive exercise brings on physical risks. These include:

- Stress fractures
- Damaged bones/joints
- Torn muscles, ligaments and tendons
- Sleep disturbance.

Losing too many calories from exercising reduces the effectiveness of the body's immune system, making you more vulnerable to illness. The dangers to mental health are similar to other addictions; excessive exercise can have a negative effect on your life, your relationships and your capacity to deal with emotions.

Some examples are provided by the 'Healthy pages' website (see Resources). One biography describes Jackie, who began working out in her 20s as a way of meeting new friends when she moved to a new town. She progressed from 'sociable exercise' such as playing tennis and squash to a more solitary exercise programme. Within a short time she was working out for six hours a day. She said she became totally obsessive and wouldn't miss a day at the gym. At the height of her addiction Jackie had a daily regime which included two hours on a bike before work, an hour's walking during her lunch hour, a two-hour run after work and a three-hour evening workout at the gym. She said that her weight dropped to 7 stone. Instead of using sport to enhance her social life, she felt she was becoming more isolated. Jackie's excessive exercise continued until she collapsed. She was admitted to hospital with cramps; she was unable to walk for ten days and had to be sedated because she could not cope without exercise.

The problem with this report is that we cannot uncover the reasons that drove Jackie to such extremes of exercise. We might guess that she also had an eating disorder, but this is not mentioned. We might wonder about why she felt so lonely and unable to make friends after her move to a new town, and about why she moved. We cannot tell whether she would be able to work through her problems because we don't know if she was able to understand why she had got into this situation. This is very often the real problem with addictions – they are used as a way of avoiding emotional difficulties, which means that before the addict can recover, they must face up to the problems they have been trying to escape and understand what drove them to addiction.

'... before the addict can recover, they must face up to the problems they have been trying to escape and understand what drove them to addiction.'

SEX ADDICTION

The power of sex as a driving force within us can bring us close to others in intimate relationships and help us form enduring bonds with a partner. But it is also possible for sex to be used to hurt or damage ourselves and others. The process of developing adult sexual bodies and acquiring the mental and emotional skills to use them safely and with respect for ourselves and others is one of the most important and momentous developments we go through as young people.

'In modern society we have a number of different views about acceptable (or unacceptable) sexual attitudes and values.'

Standards, attitudes and moral values about appropriate sexual behaviour change as societies change. For example, there used to be a 'double standard' about what young men and young women should and shouldn't do sexually (it was acceptable for men to 'do' much more than women) – but this has become less noticeable over the past 40 years. In modern society we have a number of different views about acceptable (or unacceptable) sexual attitudes and values. The range of opinions people have about heterosexuality (sexual relationships with the opposite sex), homosexuality (sexual relationships with the same sex) and monogamy (staying faithful to one partner) shows that our society has many different ways of looking at things. The media – again – has a heightened interest in and wish to communicate about the sexual activities of celebrities. We are shown everything they do, at close quarters. The lurid way in which these stories are presented encourages us both to criticise the celebrities and, sometimes, almost to admire their activities. We are supposed to think they are wrong – but at the same time, we are invited to be jealous of them and encouraged to want to imitate them.

What is addiction to sex?

Sex just cannot be avoided in our society and there are a lot of incentives to get involved in sexual activity. But for the person who is *addicted* to sex, there can be intense and extremely difficult conflicts and costs. For these people, sex serves the same function as drugs and alcohol, providing a high that is both exhilarating and numbing.

Addictive activity starts with excessive sexuality and this leads to the compulsive, irresistible seeking out of sexual activity. Fantasies of sex preoccupy and – as with other addictions – there is a progressive involvement and a vicious cycle in which sex is used to achieve good feelings and escape from bad ones, including shame, remorse, depression, anxiety and guilt. Sexual activity of this kind can be either with sexual partners or through pornographic obsessions – a field which has greatly widened through the internet.

However, we do have to be careful about how sexual addiction is defined. Treating it as a 'disease' might mean that we lose sight of the complex relationship and emotional issues which underpin sexual activities. The crucial point is that sex can be used to create a high and to avoid more depressing or worrying thoughts and feelings. Addictive sexual activity means that the other person drops out of sight as someone whose feelings and thoughts matter. This is very different from the use of sex to develop intimacy.

'... the other person drops out of sight as someone whose feelings and thoughts matter.'

What are the criteria for sexual addiction?

Sexual addiction consists of a number of behaviours which are similar to those of other addictions. These include:

■ Needing increasing amounts of sexual activity to achieve your required or desired level of pleasure

■ Feeling uncomfortable or frustrated if you have to stop being involved in sexual behaviour

■ Staying involved in sexual activity for longer than you intended

■ Wishing you could cut down and control your need for sexual behaviour

■ Spending a lot of time preparing for or recovering from sexual behaviour

■ Giving up or missing important activities (like school, work or socialising) to engage in sexual activities

■ Continuing with sexual behaviour despite knowing that it is damaging you physically and mentally.

What are the causes and effects of addiction to sex?

There are many reports by people who have felt trapped by their addictive sexual behaviour. These people commonly report that sex was the only thing they could think about, and that their desires were too strong for them to manage. They believed that sexual behaviour was a 'magical' cure for difficult feelings and states of mind – especially depression. They knew that they had difficulties and that they should seek help – possibly psychiatric help – but did not. The behaviour made them feel terrible, as it cut across other roles they had (such as being a wife or husband), and led them into a life of deceit and mistrust.

Consequences of compulsive sexual behaviour can be extreme, because other people's responses to it can be very powerful. You risk damaging your health, your finances, your career and your relationship with your family. Physical risks include sexually transmitted infections (STIs).

> **For a closer look at sex and relationships,**
> **including STIs, see**
> ***Real Life Issues: Sex and Relationships.***

INTERNET ADDICTION

The internet is a tremendous source of information and knowledge and increases the ways we can communicate with others. We rely on it more and more. The use of the internet has increased considerably during the last few years, and alongside this there have been some reports that people can 'get hooked' and develop an internet addiction. Because this is a new phenomenon, we are still finding out what it means to be addicted to the internet – and if it is valid to talk about 'internet addiction'.

What is internet addiction?

Concern about internet use focuses on the way that some people:

- Spend a lot of time on the internet – so that it is used excessively
- Use the internet as a means of taking part in traditional addictive activities in a new way – especially gambling, compulsive shopping and sex
- Show the signs of addictive patterns of behaviour in relation to the internet.

Survey results show that between 6 per cent and 10 per cent of internet users have the signs and symptoms of addiction. Young people – especially young men – are the group most likely to have problems with the internet. Children can also get into difficulties of this kind from an early age

What are the criteria for internet addiction

Dr Young from the Center for Online Addiction (see Resources) has developed a way of assessing whether someone is addicted to the internet. You can try this test online, or use the questions below which are based on the questions Dr Young asks.

1. Do you spend a lot of time thinking about your previous sessions online or looking forward to your next session?
2. Do you feel that you don't get satisfaction from the internet unless you spend increasing periods of time using it? In other words, are you spending longer and longer on the internet so that you feel satisfied?
3. Have you repeatedly tried to control, cut back or stop your internet use, but not been able to?
4. Do you stay online longer than you mean to?
5. Have you risked the loss of an important relationship, job, educational or career opportunity because of the internet?
6. Have you lied to people in order to conceal how much time you spend on the internet?
7. Do you use the internet as a way of escaping from problems or of trying to get away from feelings of helplessness, guilt, anxiety or depression?

If you answer 'yes' to more than five of these questions, there are warning signs that you probably have problems with the use of the internet.

What are the causes and effects of internet addiction?

Problems with internet use can have the same effects as any other addictive activity. There are particular areas of internet use that have caused concern – gambling pages, sex and pornographic websites, and chat rooms. The internet is particularly appealing to those who find it hard to make relationships, who are shy and withdrawn, or who find ordinary relationships unsatisfying. The internet can seem to offer an easy, alternative, 'virtual' way of relating to people. Sometimes, an internet chat room user can develop a virtual personality – which is an illusion and not like the real person.

The attraction of 'chat rooms'

One chat room user said:

'I rapidly recognised the computer was more satisfying than my relationship with my husband or daughter. I could get ample attention; my opinions were listened to and actually sought after.'

Source: BBC News 23.8.99 on www.bbc.co.uk

Addiction to the internet, or other addictions pursued by a new route?

The internet has provided new ways of getting into addictive activities – particularly the chat room. Users say that the effects can be as severe as any other addiction. One internet user described internet auctions as 'worse than cigarettes and just as expensive as gambling'. However, others have said that too many activities are being included in the idea of internet addiction. They argue that the internet is simply a different way of taking part in addictive activities which already exist – so, for example, the internet auction is really just another form of gambling.

Therefore it is important to look at what the internet is being used for, rather than classifying all time online as an internet addiction. The nature of the internet obsession must be discovered. This helps us make a distinction between a new form of addiction and a new method of following an old addiction. There are many different uses of the internet – it is not simply about 'surfing'. It can be used in a completely safe and unthreatening way – but it can also provide a new way of taking a short cut out of relationships and emotional experiences. It seems to appeal to those who see in the screen and the keyboard a solution to difficulties which then don't get faced in reality.

COPING STRATEGIES

1. Assess how far you are involved in any of the three addictive activities in this chapter. Use the criteria for each of these provided in the sections above.

2. If you are worried about your activities, then talk to someone you trust or make an appointment to see someone in a professional role, like a counsellor or psychotherapist.

3. Assess how much time you spend thinking about these activities and how much you would *not* like someone to know about your involvement and the extent of it. Remember that being honest about something you don't like about yourself is not easy.

4. If you feel you are trying to hide something from yourself and/or from others, talk to someone about it.

For more information on ways of getting out of addictions, and on how to find help, see Chapter 8.

WHAT LEADS TO ADDICTION?
Managing emotions, intimacy, disappointments and losses

Now we will look at some of the factors that might lead you to start getting involved in addictive activities. This brings together some of the points that have been made in earlier chapters – especially the idea that there are always personal events and emotional experiences (like pains and disappointments) that lead to addiction.

This chapter focuses on *the risks there are for young people in particular*, which is important because it is recognised that many addictions begin in the teenage years. Addiction is a possible outcome for a very small number of young people, but many more of you might feel, at times, that you have had a close call, or an escape. It is important to look closely at what factors can increase the risk of becoming involved in addictive activities. You are less likely to become addicted if you have:

■ Supportive structures around you – family, school, work, leisure activities

- A feeling that supportive people are interested in your thoughts, feelings and well-being
- A sense that talking about what is affecting you helps
- A belief or hope that making sense of feelings helps to change things.

You are more likely to become addicted if you have:
- A liking for getting high, excited or manic with friends, and a dislike of feeling left out of the group
- Difficulties letting go of childhood and fear of growing up, *or*
- Difficulties waiting for future adult power and responsibility and a desire to get a sense of independence and freedom from relying on parents *now*, without having to wait
- Experience of profound disappointments with others, which make you want to avoid the pain you associate with relationships.

Not everyone who fits into these categories will become addicted, but most people who get into difficulties with addiction will fit into one or more of them.

We will now focus in on the categories that increase your risk of becoming addicted.

EXCITEMENT – AN OPPORTUNITY OR A RISK?

Excitement is great, and it is very important in life. But excitement can also be precarious and lead to risk taking. Some of the energy and excitement young people have comes from a greater sense of independence and freedom, and the physical, emotional and mental developments that are taking place.

Groups of friends are very important during your teens. Often there is a build-up of excitement and risks are taken. This is in itself inevitable since taking risks is essential in life, but some people are able to take risks from a secure base and not get carried away, whereas others are not.

Excitement within a supportive group of friends

You might belong to a group of friends in which the aim of enjoyment and trying new activities takes place in a thoughtful way. These groups tend to want to look out for the safety of group members as well as to have a good time. If you are a member of a group like this, you will find that your group draws the line when something potentially harmful comes along. You can enjoy exciting times because there is safety or security in the knowledge that the group will not go too far. Though alcohol and drugs might be used by your group, this is not done in dangerous circumstances.

'You can enjoy exciting times because there is safety or security in the knowledge that the group will not go too far.'

The present and the future seem to hold exciting possibilities and opportunities to members of the group. The group accepts (but possibly doesn't mention) that parents are still needed from time to time. Parental advice and authority is still available to maintain support structures, if it is needed. Trying out drink, drugs or activities like gambling in this context is unlikely to lead to addiction.

Excitement within an unsupportive group of friends

We can contrast this with a different kind of group, one which is more vulnerable to developing addictive behaviour. These kinds of groups are unsupportive and potentially harmful. First we will look at a case study to see how this kind of group works. (The example used here is of a male group – but female groups can be very similar.)

CASE STUDY

John is 16 and he and his three friends are heavily into going out, drinking, and using cannabis – and, increasingly, cocaine. John has also started to get involved with girls. He has had a girlfriend for a month but he started to feel insecure around her, especially if she was busy and not able to see him. He talked to his friends about this and they said he should not put up with it. They encouraged him to 'dump' her. After these discussions, John impulsively got together with another girl after having a lot to drink and using cocaine. The next day he was sick – physically – and he felt angry with himself for what he had done.

John's group was beginning to use increasing quantities of drink and drugs. When John showed his concern about his girlfriend, the boys in his group didn't help him recognise his insecurity (and, probably, his jealousy). Instead, they encouraged him to blame the girl for his difficulties. John followed their advice and ended up being ill and disliking himself. This group had no time for depending on parents and any sense of limitations had been blown away. The members of John's group denied any need for others, and were swept away with a belief that they could do anything they wished.

When this kind of thinking takes hold, people are used rather than related to. Tender feelings – such as feeling vulnerable, feeling in need of reassurance from others, and being intimate – may be criticised and ignored because they are feared. A vicious circle can be set up where 'using' people in relationships leads to bad feelings, which leads to feeling no good, which leads to using people to make you feel better, and so on.

When you feel, like John, that you dislike yourself for something you have done, there is an opportunity to think about things. John was able to allow an adult he trusted to help him because he was able to share his feeling of not liking himself – and this led him to realise that he did not really want to carry on behaving in the same way. But it is hard to leave a group like this and John had to face some difficult feelings to make a stand to be different. His vulnerability was that he found that he could not easily give up on the excitement offered by the group, and for some time it was not clear which way he would go. John did eventually find the strength to be true to his real feelings and give up his addictive habits.

BEING FEARFUL OF GROWING UP

You undergo a lot of changes during your teenage years, and these can be difficult to cope with. Being anxious about growing up is healthy! Sometimes, it can seem difficult to leave childhood – you want to cling on to childhood ways of relating to others, *and* kick start adulthood, both at the same time. The next case study shows how, when circumstances have been adverse, the fear of growing up can lead to addictive activities.

FACT BOX

Excitement and mania: what's the difference?

Excitement and manic states of mind are quite close together, but also poles apart. Excitement is a good feeling which comes from growth and good things happening. A manic state of mind involves a much more destructive sense of triumphing over those on whom you depend and rely on. In this state of mind you feel that depending on others makes you feel small and humiliated. So you reject others' care for you and avoid the possibility of feeling small and vulnerable. You will want to be independent in every way and always in control – but this is not realistic and in the end not good for you.

CASE STUDY

Alan, 17, had a close group of friends who used cannabis and ecstasy frequently. He became depressed and very scared after taking these drugs. He started to have panic attacks. His father left home when he was ten and his grandmother, whom he loved dearly, died soon after this. He was haunted by these losses, and was scared of growing up, of becoming a man. Because he was stuck with losses he couldn't get over, he couldn't leave childhood and take up more adult-like responsibilities. Though talented, he did not succeed at school and he started to take drugs. He complained about being dependent upon his mother and did not accept her authority or concern.

Alan had a bad reaction to taking drugs, similar to Simon (whom we discussed in Chapter 2). The encounter with drugs brought to the surface difficulties that he found hard to face. Alan was very fearful of growing up after the losses he suffered in his childhood. Alan needed the structure, attention and thoughtfulness that a child-and-adolescent psychotherapist could provide to help him recognise the fears that he had been unable to see or deal with himself. Through his psychotherapy he began to recognise and give names to the emotions that he had run away from, and which he could not describe for himself. This is an essential part of the therapeutic process: it makes coping with your emotions – something which you must be able to do if you are to manage without drugs – more bearable.

FACT BOX

Psychotherapy, or psychological therapy, means changing your behaviour, attitudes, states of mind, and underlying conflicts through talking to a trained therapist. There are many different forms of psychotherapy, but all have in common the aim of bringing about change through talking, rather than using medication. Psychotherapy usually involves regular sessions – once a week or more often is usual – for a period of time.

Now let us look at another case study:

CASE STUDY

Yolanda had a sexual relationship with her boyfriend when she was 14. She began this relationship with great excitement, but in ways which she could not really understand, she found that she felt ashamed, guilty and very anxious. She felt that she was not in control of herself and her feelings. She stopped the sexual part of the relationship, persuaded her boyfriend to stay friends with her, and daydreamed that she would marry him when she felt old enough. But her idea of marriage was that she would have someone who looked after her – more like a parent than a husband. Without really knowing why, Yolanda started to eat less, cutting out some types of food, particularly meat. This behaviour increased until her weight went down and she had amenorrhoea (loss of periods). Without being able to know it herself, or put it into words, Yolanda created in herself a sense of a child who was not growing up. Yolanda's fear of growing up was centred round the idea that she would no longer be looked after, like a child by parents. She didn't really know this herself – or only had glimpses of what she was feeling.

Sometimes, attempts to take up more adult ways of relating to people can make us very anxious. In Yolanda's case, the experience was too much and she tried to return to childhood ways of being and relating. Perhaps Yolanda had not been able to wait to start her relationship – perhaps she was not emotionally ready for it and because of this she got frightened and her development was put on hold. Like Alan, Yolanda propelled herself into an adult-like state as a way of avoiding the pains of waiting, and this led to disappointment and misery. She too was helped by psychotherapy, where she was able to begin to understand for herself the meaning beneath her experiences – to understand that she had shot out of childhood because she was fearful of leaving it.

DISAPPOINTMENTS IN RELATIONSHIPS

Often, the teenage years are seen as a time when you don't get on with your parents and other adults. There are different levels of 'not getting on' – some arguments, for example, 'clear the air'. Others can be more painful, but we are still able to keep our love and respect for others even when we are upset with them. On the other hand, some arguments threaten to break down our relationships completely, which may lead to the feeling that others don't love us anymore.

Arguments may not be the only difficulty you face. If you have a difficult home life then you are much more likely to get involved in addictive activities, especially where there are problems with family relationships. Examples of this kind of problem include:

- The death of a parent
- Parent(s) with mental health difficulties
- A lot of conflict between parents (either whilst together or separated)
- Parent(s) with problems of their own (including misuse of alcohol or drugs)
- Being abused by a parent (physically, sexually or emotionally)
- Being bullied by peers.

> **For information on bullying, see**
> ***Real Life Issues: Bullying.***

These experiences are likely to increase feelings of rejection, abandonment, anger and rage. Often, it can be difficult to identify these feelings in yourself and to link them with the things that have happened.

When relationships are difficult or threatened in the ways described above, you might feel like no one understands you, and that you can't confide in anyone. This means that you are stuck with your feelings and don't know where to turn. It might seem that if you do talk to someone, it will only make you feel worse – so you may feel that there is no point opening up to someone else and it's better to sort yourself out by yourself. If this is how you feel a lot or most of the time, you will be more likely to experience difficulties and turn to addictive activities.

CASE STUDY

George is 16. His father died recently after a short illness. George's parents had not got on well and his mother had difficulties of her own. She had been depressed for a long time and sometimes she had to go into hospital for help and treatment. At times, George's mother felt suicidal. When his father died, George felt responsible for his mother as well as worried about her. He was not able to study and he missed taking his GCSE exams. He spent a lot of time on the internet, and he started to drink heavily and use cannabis. George was at risk of developing an addiction. He felt very burdened by the difficult situation in his family and the feeling that he couldn't get his own life into gear. He felt that it was hard to be confident in social situations and hopeless about making a difference to his life. We will see how George was helped to find his way through this in Chapter 8.

In these circumstances, the risk of turning to addictive activities stems from:

■ Feeling that you lack confidence in ordinary circumstances

- Finding it easier to get a sense that someone notices you in a group which is doing drugs
- Not being able to talk about yourself with others and perhaps having to hide how you really feel
- Feeling left out of ordinary conversations with other young people
- Feeling that you can't manage relationships at all and withdrawing from emotional attachment to avoid feeling humiliated, rejected or abandoned.

DEPENDENCY: A GOOD OR A BAD THING?

We have come back to the important theme of dependency. All relationships require trust and an ability to depend on others. Feeling dependent does not feel bad if we can trust others to respond to our needs. We can allow ourselves to be vulnerable – to show our feelings and let others know what troubles us – more easily if we can let ourselves rely on others. Being dependent is the basis of intimate relationships, which we all need throughout our lives in order to experience ourselves as real and important.

At the same time, we have to accept that we cannot own or have exclusive rights to another person – they have their own life and needs and do not exist just to satisfy our needs and wishes. Sometimes it can be very difficult to share someone important to us with others, and with the other things they are interested in. We get jealous and possessive. But we all have to learn that other people are independent of us even if we depend on them.

For a closer look at how to handle relationships, see *Real Life Issues: Sex & Relationships*

CASE STUDY

Elizabeth felt she had 'had it' with her parents and her foster carers. She felt she had been pushed from pillar to post and it was certainly true that she had been through a very difficult time. She still longed to be with her parents, especially her father whom she hoped one day she would be able to go back and live with. But, as she often said, he was just so unreliable. Elizabeth didn't do what anyone told her to, and she couldn't stand it when someone tried to talk to her as though she was a child. She would 'blow', furiously, at the slightest thing. She went out a lot and had a succession of boyfriends whom she dumped before they could dump her. She was always the first to suggest a party and the last one to go home. She took a lot of drugs – especially cannabis, ecstasy and cocaine. She thought this was great and that she was in charge instead of being made to feel small by the way her parents and foster parents treated her. But she lost control of her drug taking. She overdosed and was admitted to hospital.

Elizabeth reached a crisis when she overdosed because she had to realise at that point that she was not in control. Although this was an awful situation it did offer an opportunity, which was not there when she was 'doing her own thing' and feeling she had the power to do anything she wanted. We will see how Elizabeth was able to regain a sense of balance and development in the next chapter.

Elizabeth was attempting to rely on drugs instead of her relationships with other people. But dependency on an addictive activity, when it is in full sway, is far more overpowering and damaging than any relationship; an addiction can truly eat you up. Sometimes people think that through addiction you can avoid the uncertainties and pains of relating to and being dependent on others. But addiction is the most unreliable of all dependencies – it always provides pain and never offers growth. Addictive activities offer a kind of terrible delight – and a terrible dependence.

The next chapter will look at ways of breaking this dependence on the addictive activity and replacing it with more healthy forms of dependence – on support from other people.

SUMMARY: WHERE DO YOU STAND?

In this chapter, we have seen that some young people can be vulnerable to developing addictions. Supportive relationships form an essential structure that helps to avoid this happening. They make it possible to face life's difficulties, regulate emotions, manage closeness in relationships and overcome disappointments and losses. When supportive relationships, in the present and the past, have been difficult to maintain, we are all more vulnerable to difficulties, including addictions.

CHAPTER EIGHT:

GETTING OUT OF ADDICTIONS
Facing yourself and changing your mindset

In this chapter we will look at some of the many kinds of help available for people who have become addicted. There are many different views about the most effective ways of helping people to recover from addiction.

RECOVERY, RELAPSE AND MANAGING CONFLICT

The main thing to remember is that, just like getting into addiction, coming out of addiction is a process. The term **recovery** is often used to describe someone stopping an addictive activity. It is a useful term, except that it is too simple. It is more helpful to think about the way someone moves away from addictive states of mind, which drive them towards addictive activity. **Relapse** is another such term, meaning that the addictive activity has been started up again. Both recovery and relapse refer to the behaviour, and not to the underlying inner conflict that may be causing it. We have seen that all addictions involve a conflict between a wish to continue the activity (or feeling unable to stop it) and the knowledge that it is doing harm. It is very difficult for an addict to recognise and understand this conflict – but once they have done so, they may find it possible to seek support to help them stop the addictive activity.

In these cases, the treatment for addiction may start after a lot of time has been spent thinking it over, and some trial actions have already been taken by the addict.

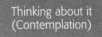
Thinking about it
(Contemplation)

Doing something about it
(Action)

In other cases, the process of moving from contemplation to action can be much faster. For example, addicts often reach crisis point – 'rock bottom' – which leads to a sudden, desperate wish to change. This is what happened to Elizabeth, whom we met in Chapter 7. Elizabeth's overdose frightened her, and also undermined her feeling that she was in control. When she realised she was not in control of her drug use she experienced all the feelings she had been trying to avoid – especially the feeling that she needed others and was hurt by them. Having a crisis like this meant she felt desperate for some help. She was able to obtain this from psychotherapy and from her foster parents, whom she stopped seeing in such a negative way.

WAYS OF TACKLING ADDICTION

In the previous chapter we looked at how addictions involve dependency. In order to get out of an addiction, this dependency needs to be broken and replaced with other, more healthy types of dependency on other people. Different addictions and states of addiction need different treatments to achieve this. Treatments can focus on the addictive activity, the person or their environment. Let us look at the different ways that an addiction can be overcome.

Tackling physical dependency

There are two main ways of addressing the chemical aspect of dependency. One is to stop the addictive activity completely – to go 'cold turkey' as it is sometimes called. This **detoxifies** the body, clearing it of the chemicals it has become addicted to. This can lead to side-effects known as **withdrawal symptoms**. Tony Adams, whose account of his alcohol addiction was discussed in Chapter 1, shows the physical effects of withdrawal.

The second method is to replace the drug with a similar but apparently less harmful one, often through prescription. For example:

- Methadone may be prescribed for heroin addicts, either to help reduce the effects of withdrawal or to stabilise the individual
- Nicotine substitutes are now widely recommended for giving up smoking.

NHS drug dependency units or community drug teams provide a course of treatment. These treatments should always be accompanied by care from nursing staff and doctors. It is important that treatment is given by a service specialising in working with young people.

CASE STUDY

Jane, whom we discussed in Chapter 2, was addicted to heroin and dependent on cocaine. She was referred by a drug action team to a unit which specialised in working with young people. Here she was given drugs on prescription to help with her heroin addiction. She went to the centre several times a week, and saw members of the professional team. She was given a prescription and her use of drugs was monitored. She could see a counsellor twice a week and discuss her drug use, her current situation and her thoughts about her life – past, present and future. This helped her regain some control through understanding. Treatment can be highly effective, and many people with drug problems can be helped. Jane is making an effort to use treatment in order to become one of these people.

Jane was in very severe difficulties. The centre provided her with both a structure and somewhere to talk in an environment which was non-judgemental, but realistic about the need to change. Change for

FACT BOX

Providing help for young people

It is important to realise that the kind of treatment that helps young people can be quite different from what might be best for adults. The government has become aware of this and has been trying to make services more suitable for young people. There are 150 local Drug Action Teams (DAT) who have responsibilities for organising services which are sensitive to the needs of young people. There is a national drug strategy, and education about drugs is an important part of this, aiming to prevent young people becoming addicted in the first place.

someone in Jane's position is not easy. She needs both structure and attachment to the team of workers to help her. This leads on to the second important aspect of tackling addiction, which looks at the psychological as well as the physical side of dependency.

CHANGING YOUR MINDSET

Reducing addictive activity means changing your attitudes – the way you think, feel and relate to others. It might mean changing your lifestyle and friendship groups and coming to terms with your life so far. It means getting to understand the personal reasons for addictive activity. To make these changes you may get help from mental health services. Treatment for addictive activities needs three conditions:

- A sound and firm structure for help. This can be a regular session with a counsellor or psychotherapist or regular meetings each week with members of a team of professionals. Sometimes it is difficult to stop the addictive activity in your family or peer group. Going into hospital can sometimes be necessary to help you start to give up the addictive activity in a supportive setting
- The opportunity to talk about yourself within the overall structure
- A commitment from the addicted person to try to change.

There are many therapeutic approaches available, and mental health services have to provide a range of them. Different people respond to different approaches – it is a matter of personal style and preference. The two main approaches for difficulties of an addictive nature are cognitive therapies and psychodynamic (or interpersonal) therapies. Having a therapeutic relationship helps you to rebuild your ability to have relationships with other people.

FACT BOX

Different kinds of therapy
There are many different kinds of psychological therapy, or psychotherapy, which aim to bring about change through purposeful talking to a trained therapist.

Cognitive therapies look at the way you think about the addictive activity and about yourself. They aim to change the ways of thinking and perceiving that you have built up around the addiction, and in your life so far.

Psychodynamic (or interpersonal) therapies look at the underlying difficulties which have led to the addiction; they aim to address problems you may have in the ways you experience relationships, past hurts and grievances, and problems in recognising and modifying emotions.

The process of getting help for an addictive activity can be painful. You have to really get to grips with what has brought you into this state and to face things. Sometimes therapy is difficult *because* it involves relating to someone else – the therapist. Relating is not easy for most people with addictions. A number of the subjects of the case studies in this book have been helped by psychotherapy, but it is not a magical solution. Both the subject and the therapist need to work hard.

CASE STUDY

George, for example, whose situation was described in Chapter 7, found psychotherapy helpful – but he also found it difficult and struggled to keep going with it. George's emotional difficulty, which led to his misuse of drugs, was that he wanted to escape from the demands of others, especially his mother's difficulties, and he was overwhelmed by the worry he felt for her. His therapy tried to help him feel concerned, and less overwhelmed. This meant that he had to develop a capacity to care for himself. Unless you care for yourself first, it is impossible to care for other people without feeling overwhelmed. To feel able to care for yourself, you have to recognise having been cared for in some way. George was able to recognise that he was being cared for by his therapist. His therapist remembered what George had told him, which helped George feel that the therapist was thinking about him and interested in him. He was then able to remember times his father had cared for him when he was alive, and the way his mother cared, even though she had many difficulties of her own. He could also feel angry with the limitations of his therapy. It could not magically repair what had happened to him. Because he could think about these feelings, he was able to begin to bear his rage about events and problems in his family. In this way, the therapeutic relationship deepened his understanding of himself and his ability to control his feelings and his relationships with others. George got a girlfriend for the first time and started to train for a career.

Not everyone can make such good use of therapy. It is not a 'fix'. Sometimes the involvement in addictive activities is so hard to control that they are returned to (known as a relapse). On the other hand, some people start to get themselves out of addiction by their own efforts – by making a decision to stop. The wish to stop and the effort put into stopping is indeed important and no therapy can succeed without the cooperation of the patient.

So it is also possible to get out of an addiction without using professional help – but not without help from some other people. We saw in the previous chapter that we must have people around us who we can depend on, so that we no longer depend on the addiction. Perhaps friends and understanding adults can help and support you. It is crucial to find someone you can speak honestly to. Being honest with yourself and others is a sign that you can face overcoming addiction because dishonesty with yourself and others is a characteristic of an addictive state of mind. There is dishonesty in every addiction. Other people and reliable structures – whether from a therapist or from your family or friends – are crucial. But you must also realise that recovery from addiction starts with you – with your wish to help yourself. Once you realise this you will be able to use those around you to get the support you need to recover.

'It is crucial to find someone you can speak honestly to.'

TALKING ABOUT IT IS BETTER

The website 'Talk to Frank' (see Resources) says that 'Drugs are illegal – Talking about them isn't'. The message is that talking about your involvement with drugs and other addictive activities is the best way of getting them under control.

Who can you talk to?

Talking honestly with friends, family members, supportive and trusted adults is helpful, though it can be difficult because it means facing yourself and what other people might think and feel about you.

Getting professional help is another way of talking about addictive activities. You can access professional support in several different ways:
- If you are in school, you can talk to the school counsellor or the Special Needs Coordinator (SENCO)
- You can make an appointment with your doctor (GP) who will be able to refer you to appropriate services. GPs now have good links with new 'outreach' services in primary care and with Child and Adolescent Mental Health Services (CAMHS) which offer counselling and psychotherapeutic services.

If you have a problem with drug use, you can also get help from:
- Street drugs agencies: most areas have 'street agencies'. They are also sometimes called 'open access' projects or community drug services
- Drug dependency units: these are usually in or next to a hospital and offer advice, treatment and information about suitable services
- The 'Talk to Frank' website: you can send an e-mail to this website, or use the search facility to access your local services.

The combination of talking and having a reliable, regular structure are the two factors that can lead to overcoming addictive activities and states of mind. This means talking honestly and facing your feelings, and also being honest with someone else who is interested in your well-being and who recognises that you need a reliable structure in your life. Facing the truth is never easy – but it is necessary, and can be rewarding!

SUMMARY

This chapter has examined ways of tackling addiction and breaking dependency on it. The aim has been to present a hopeful but realistic picture. It is important to think of recovery as a process which involves making changes to the way you think about yourself and relate to others.

Throughout the book, we have placed great emphasis on the importance of other people and getting help through talking to others. Trying to develop relationships in which you can think about your feelings is crucial.

By getting to know more about the reasons for addictions and their effects you are better informed now and probably more able to find ways of avoiding these activities. You may also be able to help friends and others. If you are unfortunate enough to have to deal with the problems of an addiction, hopefully this book will have helped you understand more about what it is that you are going through, and the examples of others might help you feel less unusual. The process of recovery is a tough one, but one which deserves everything you can give it!

'The process of recovery is a tough one, but one which deserves everything you can give it!'

RESOURCES

In this section you will find details of useful organisations, books and websites.

GENERAL

Addictions.co.uk www.addictions.co.uk
This website is sponsored by Priory Healthcare, and gives information on all addictive activities – it starts from the view that addictions can be formed from any activity which allows people to escape from life. It has a young person's section.

Excessive Appetites: A Psychological View of Addictions by Jim Orford (Wiley, 2001)
A good, academic sourcebook, which is recommended to anyone who wants to go deeply into the subject.

HIT www.hit.org.uk
HIT delivers effective interventions on drugs, alcohol, sexual health, community safety and other public health concerns.
Hanover House, Hanover Street
Liverpool L1 3DZ

Tel: 0870 990 9702
Fax: 0870 990 9703

YoungMinds www.youngminds.org.uk
An organisation that promotes the welfare of children and young
people. The website has a young person's section and provides a great
deal of information about all aspects of mental health, together with
comprehensive links.

DRUGS AND ALCOHOL

Addicted by Tony Adams with Ian Ridley (Collins Willow, 1998)
A very candid account of addiction to alcohol, and recovering from it.

Adfam www.adfam.org.uk
Adfam provides confidential support and information for the families
and friends of drug users. Information on local services and a range of
publications are available from the website.
Waterbridge House, 32-36 Loman Street
London SE1 0EH
Tel: 020 7928 8898
Fax: 020 7928 8923
Email: admin@adfam.org.uk

Drink Aware www.drinkaware.co.uk
This website is run by the Portman Group, and aims to promote
sensible drinking. It includes an alcohol unit calculator (using real drink
brands), and advice about what's in which drinks.

DrugScope UK www.drugscope.org.uk
An independent website, with comprehensive coverage of drug issues
including a section for ethnic minorities (in 11 languages). The

organisation also publishes books. *The Druglink Guide to Drugs* (2004) is especially useful in providing a detailed account of all psychoactive drugs.

Release www.release.org.uk
Release offers a range of specialist services to professionals and to the public concerning drugs and the law.
388 Old Street
London EC1V 9LT
Helpline: 0845 4500 215
Fax: 020 7729 2599
Email: ask@release.org.uk

Tackling Drugs www.drugs.gov.uk
A government website which explains the drugs strategy and includes all the addresses of the local Drug Action Centres.

Talk to Frank www.talktofrank.com
The website 'Talk to Frank' has been set up by the government to provide an internet base for talking about drugs. It is designed for young people between 11 and 21 and their parents. You can write an email to Frank and receive a confidential reply offering advice and suggestions. Frank will never send an email without you asking him to. The website has a lot of information, particularly about Class A drugs and about teenagers and drugs.

GAMBLING

Gamblers Anonymous (UK) www.gamblersanonymous.org.uk
Gamblers Anonymous is a fellowship of men and women who have joined together to do something about their own gambling problem and to help other compulsive gamblers do the same.

PO Box 88, London SW10 0EU

Tel: National & London: 08700 50 88 80; Sheffield: 0114 262 0026;

Manchester: 0161 976 5000; Birmingham: 0121 233 1335;

Glasgow: 0141 630 1033; Belfast: 028 7135 1329

GamCare www.gamcare.org.uk

GamCare, a registered charity, is one of the leading authorities on the provision of information, advice and practical help in addressing the social impact of gambling.

2&3 Baden Place, Crosby Row

London SE1 1YW

Tel: 020 7378 5200

Helpline: 0845 6000 133 (24 hour, 7 days a week)

Fax: 020 7378 5237

Email: info@gamcare.org.uk

EATING DISORDERS

Adios Barbie www.adiosbarbie.com

A website which uses features, articles and readers' comments to develop positive thinking about the diverse ways we look and criticises the current pressure to be thin.

Eating disorders www.something-fishy.org

There are a number of useful websites for eating disorders. This one promotes awareness about eating disorders and offers information relevant to those with an eating disorder, family and friends.

Eating Disorder Association (EDA)

EDA provides information and help on all aspects of eating disorders including anorexia nervosa, bulimia nervosa, binge eating disorder and related eating disorders.

103 Prince of Wales Road
Norwich NR1 1DW
Adults' Helpline: 0845 634 1414 (open Mon–Fri 8:30–20:30; Sat 13:00–16:30)
Email: helpmail@edauk.com
Youthline (for callers 18 and under): 0845 634 7650 (open Mon–Fri 16:00–18:30; Sat 13:00–16:30)
Email: talkback@edauk.com
Text-phone Service: 01603 753322 (open 8:30 to 20:30 weekdays)

Body Mass Calculators
From the Food Standards Agency:
www.eatwell.gov.uk/healthy_diet/healthy_weight/bmicalculator/
From the Health Education Board for Scotland:
www.hebs.scot.nhs.uk/Learningcentre/obesity/bmi.cfm

EXCESSIVE EXERCISE
Healthypages www.healthypages.net
Has information and articles about healthy living and addictive activities including excessive exercise.

INTERNET ADDICTION
Center for Online Addiction www.netaddiction.com
Provides information about internet addictions.